ELEMENTS

of Wit

ELEMENTS
of Wit

MASTERING THE ART
OF BEING INTERESTING

◆ ◆ ◆

Benjamin Errett

Illustrations by Sarah Lazarovic

A PERIGEE BOOK

A PERIGEE BOOK
Published by the Penguin Group
Penguin Group (USA) LLC
375 Hudson Street, New York, New York 10014

USA • Canada • UK • Ireland • Australia • New Zealand • India • South Africa • China

penguin.com

A Penguin Random House Company

ELEMENTS OF WIT

ISBN: 978-0-399-16910-6

First edition: October 2014

PRINTED IN THE UNITED STATES OF AMERICA

10 9 8 7 6 5 4 3 2

Text design by Tiffany Estreicher

To my children, Helena and Theodore,
without whose never-failing sympathy and
encouragement this book would have been
finished in half the time*

CONTENTS

Why Wit?

There you are, in a big sales meeting. The client makes a weak joke in your direction and the boss looks your way. Say something. Say anything. Well, not just anything—you need something clever but innocuous, smart enough to show your intelligence without showing off, something funny but not a joke. You don't want to be offensive, snide or holier than thou. If this were a game of tennis, you'd simply want to keep the ball in play. At this moment, what you need is wit.

Unfortunately, in the time it took to read those sentences, your window of opportunity has slammed shut. The pregnant pause gave birth to awkward silence, and a colleague coughed, or spoke up, or dropped a pen. The spotlight has shifted, at least for now. But this will happen again, one day. A moment like this will be presented to you and you alone. You can once more hope for a distraction. (Or maybe hire your coughing colleague to follow you around, hacking you out of difficult situations.)

Alternately, you can respond with just the right words at just the right time, putting the client at ease, impressing the boss, brightening the room and showing yourself to be in command of the situation.

OK, so maybe you don't attend sales meetings. You're self-employed. You avoid people who cough. Still, wouldn't you choose the second option? Of course you would. But how?

This book is how. It's also why, and most important, it's who.

What if one of the Great Wits had been sitting in your chair in that moment of need? Say Oscar Wilde, green carnation in lapel and all, was prepared to offer a rejoinder on your behalf. Why, it would be like when Alvy Singer enlisted Marshall McLuhan to quiet a loudmouth in *Annie Hall*.

To be clear, the physical reanimation of the illustrious dead is sadly not the subject of this book. Instead, it's a deep dive into the character traits of the Great Wits, those names seen most often at the end of aphorisms and quips, with one express purpose: To find out how they did it. What skills, talents, flaws and peccadillos fixed their wit in the popular imagination? And—this is where you, sitting in your little sales meeting, praying for inspiration, come in—how can a modern reader learn from these individuals?

In some cases, the lessons are almost entirely what not to do. There are Great Wits who led horrid lives, the wisecracks coming at the price of just about everything else. Can you subtract the substance abuse, the cruelty, the thwarted aspirations and the abject misery to leave behind a facility for sparkling epigrams? This book says, you know what? Sure you can.

A Brief Socratic Dialogue That Includes Finger Foods

We open on the Author's sitting room. You sit side by side in tastefully upholstered wingback chairs. The fireplace is crackling away and there is still frost on your respective martini glasses. The Reader is briefly surprised by the transportive power of words—a moment ago you were thumbing through this book on the new and noteworthy table at the bookseller, but maybe that's the Tanqueray talking. You regain composure and repeat your question.

READER: What's the point of wit?
AUTHOR: The sharp end, the part that hurts.

READER: You know what I mean. What's it for?
AUTHOR: It's for intelligent conversation, sharp thinking,

laughter, truth and human civilization. But what's more important is what it's against.

READER: Which is?

AUTHOR: Regurgitated thought, talking points, doublespeak, stagnation and dullness.

READER: So it's for good things and against bad things? These days, who isn't?

AUTHOR: Ah, but wit is the horse that best pulls that crowded bandwagon.

READER: And you're saying she's been put out to pasture by mistake?

AUTHOR: Exactly. But not by mistake, really.

READER: So what do we need to bring her back, aside from another drink?

The Author swallows the last drops of his martini, fetches your empty glass, passes you a plate of deviled eggs and walks over to the well-stocked beverage cart.

READER: Less vermouth this time, please.

AUTHOR: Of course. Now what I mean to say is that wit hasn't simply been gently forgotten. It's been misunderstood, redefined and twisted into a meaningless word. Its definition is now barely defined.

READER: So *who*'s made wit so meaningless, *what* did it used to mean, *where* did we go wrong, *when* was this alleged golden age of wit and *why* should we care?

AUTHOR: You forgot *how*.

READER: How will you answer my previous questions?

AUTHOR: The insecure made it meaningless; it once meant good sense that sparkles; we killed it by accusing it of cruelty and memorizing bad jokes instead; it was ascendant during the Enlightenment, but perhaps also during the 1920s; and we should care because it's the best possible use of our brains.

READER: The best possible use of our brains? What about curing diseases? Repartee isn't much use against the Ebola virus.

AUTHOR: OK, "best" may be a subjective term there. But wit, if we return to its original definition—and perhaps dress it up a bit for the twenty-first century—can get us to all sorts of discoveries.

READER: And that original definition is good sense that sparkles?

AUTHOR: In brief, yes. That's how the seventeenth-century French thinker Dominique Bouhours defined "bel esprit," literally "beautiful spirit." Or as thinkers like Johnson, Hazlitt and Coleridge defined it in England at about the same time, it's the rapid combination of disparate ideas to create delight. Our definition is even simpler: Wit is spontaneous creativity.

The Reader helps self to a third martini and a fistful of gherkins.

READER: So you're saying wit is creativity?

AUTHOR: Wit is the ability to be creative on the fly, to

combine ideas in conversation, to make connections quickly and with joy, and in doing so make life worth living.

READER: Wit is necessary, sparkly, the opposite of jokes and similar to creativity? I can see why you say it's misunderstood.

AUTHOR: The three-martini introduction probably isn't helping. Shall we return to the book?

READER: *(Hiccups and nods appreciatively.)*

Defining Our Terms

Wit is, for our purposes, spontaneous creativity. Note that this definition doesn't specify that wit is true, or that it's funny. We might add the words "to create delight" on the end of that definition, but on some level all creativity is delightful to a thinking mind.

How did we get to this definition? As we've seen, there were some brilliant Enlightenment thinkers who set out inspiring meanings for the word "wit." The problem is, they were *too* good. They made wit sound like the best thing ever, the ultimate compliment and the pinnacle of human achievement. Soon, that meant everything good was wit; any good idea, clever remark or clear thought. Wit, as C. S. Lewis writes in his essay on the word, "suffered the worst fate any word has to fear; it became the fashionable term of approval among critics." This led to it being further twisted, its meanings conflated until it was "semantically null." Now it has come to rest as a vague subset of humor, used to describe certain movies or books but rarely in any specific way.

That didn't totally happen with the word "wit" when used to describe a person. If you refer to someone as a Wit, your meaning will generally be understood. Now, we arrive at the concept of creativity from the Enlightenment definitions of wit as an attribute, but we can also get there as we talk about the Wit as a person—though by a very different path.

There is a small body of research from the 1960s on the character of the Wit, much of it coming from a mysterious U.S. military research group known as Serendipity Associates. The U.S. Air Force, it seems, was very interested in harnessing the power of the Wit. It funded a series of papers by this group to examine who wits are and how they behave. In 1963's "The Wit in Large and Small Established Groups," the Air Force found that "deliberate wits are associated with higher morale and greater role clarity and efficiency in small groups." A year later, in "The Wit and His Group," a study of two six-person groups found that wits "expressed a positive self-image," and that groups containing wits "evaluated the group experience favorably" and "did better on a problem-solving task than others."

And in 1965's "Wit, Creativity and Sarcasm," researchers made the jump to creative thinking, finding that wit and creativity were positively correlated, and that while the Wit was not an effective leader in a group, having one around generally made everyone better at problem solving. With no real evidence to support this idea, I'd like to think that NASA used this research to choose the members of the Apollo missions, and that when the

Navy assembles a team of SEALs for a perilous mission into enemy territory, it always includes at least one happy warrior. This would explain the presence of lovable doofus Chris Pratt in the otherwise lovable-doofus-free *Zero Dark Thirty*.

Further research solidified the link to creativity—it's "the best single significant predictor of wit," Dr. John F. Clabby wrote in 1980's "The Wit: A Personality Analysis"—but from that point, the mention of wit in psychology research all but stops. At about the same time, there's a marked increase in the study of creativity. Studies of how and why creativity happens were refined into concepts with names like divergent thinking (generating many different ideas) and conceptual blending (bringing those ideas together), both of which have a more than passing resemblance to the old "rapid combination of disparate ideas."

The research interest in creativity intensifies after 1990, as that's when U.S. student scores on the Torrance Tests of Creative Thinking stopped improving. In the field of IQ testing, there's something called the Flynn Effect, in which average IQ scores creep up by about three points a decade. No one's sure exactly why this happens, but the most interesting and broad explanations have to do with the effects of modern life on our minds: We have to be smarter just to work our smartphones.

The Torrance Tests had similar findings, but only until 1990. At that point, scores start decreasing; year after year, people actually become less creative. Why 1990? It's unclear, and while it almost certainly has nothing to do with the fact that *Dances with Wolves* beat *Goodfellas* for the best picture Oscar that year, we will make a passing mention of that travesty anyway.

As of 2010, scores were still falling, hence a *Newsweek* cover story titled "The Creativity Crisis." Why is this happening? The usual culprits of TV and video games are often blamed, as is the education system with its standardized tests. But as with the Flynn Effect, no one's really sure. The one certainty about this news is that if you're a social scientist looking to have your research funded, it can't hurt to highlight the word "creativity," and maybe throw in some neurobiology while you're at it.

And therein lies the problem with talking about creativity: It's a huge subject with many working theories and even more definitions. The act of creation is exactly what a sculptor does, for instance, but creative thinking is just as necessary for genetic researchers and CEOs.

A worthy parsing of what creativity means comes from Mihaly Csikszentmihalyi, a psychology professor who wrote a book called, creatively enough, *Creativity*. As he explains, there are "three different phenomena that can be legitimately called by this name." In inverse order, he discusses people who've dramatically changed the culture, people who "experience the world in novel and original ways" and then the group we're most interested in here:

The first usage, widespread in ordinary conversation, refers to persons who express unusual thoughts, who are interesting and stimulating— in short, to people who appear to be unusually bright. A brilliant conversationalist, a person with varied interests and a quick mind, may be called creative in this sense. Unless they also contribute something of permanent significance, I refer to people of this sort as brilliant rather than creative—and by and large I don't say much about them in this book.

We'll say plenty about them in this book, and the distinction Csikszentmihalyi makes is an important one. By his definition, some of the Wits we'll meet are merely brilliant, some are creative and some are both. But what of those who may have created something of permanent significance but were much more dazzling in conversation? Or how about our contemporaries, those whose work can't yet be tested for permanence because they've only just finished it? We'll stick to creativity in our definition, and if this book helps you become spontaneously brilliant instead of spontaneously creative, we'll assume you won't demand your money back.

So think of wit as a backdoor into creativity, then. It's not the sort that will help you create a Fortune 500 company, a poem that speaks to a generation or the next dance craze, at least not by itself. But it will help you make the most of daily conversations and interactions and feel more at home in the world. And who knows? That could be the first step toward something bigger.

A Question of Timing

But what about the spontaneity part of our definition?

Calling it spontaneous creativity would seem to put a premium on wit in conversation, since wit on the printed page is impossible to certify as impromptu. By spontaneity, we mean creativity that appears to happen at the speed of thought and in the moment. The key words here are *"appears to* happen." Are stand-up comedians witty? The best are, sure, even though we know they've painstakingly honed their material. Wit can shine on the printed page, though even at this late stage in the history of books, it takes many months for them to pass from writer to reader. In a movie or television show, the wittiest dialogue may have been improvised—it's a badge of honor for actors to ad-lib a great line—but it's far more likely to have been scripted and rehearsed with great care. And even on talk-show interviews, we know the best quips have been drawn out of the guests in green-room interviews, with the hosts prompted to say, "So I hear you're having trouble with your pet iguana" as though it's a perfectly natural subject of conversation.

We should also note that wit need not even be in language: In art and especially graphic design, visual wit is among the highest of ideals. To borrow the title of an excellent book on the subject, wit in this context—as perhaps in all contexts—should create "a smile in the mind." Take, for instance, the FedEx logo. Even if you've never used the courier, you can probably see its trademark font and colors in  your mind's eye. But did you ever notice the arrow hidden between the "E" and the "x"? This nearly subliminal message—a perfect symbol for its service—is famous in design circles for being hidden in plain sight. And indeed, your mind smiles when you see it. Unless you're a graphic designer, though, this won't directly help you master the art of being interesting, so in this book we'll keep our focus on verbal wit.

The key in all of the above instances of wit is the perception of spontaneity, the impression that the lines were dashed off, not

> *Spontaneity is entirely in the ear of the beholder.*

labored over. This definitely doesn't mean they actually have to be spontaneous; in fact, we will see that most of the Great Wits were anything but. The great conversation retorts were very often rehearsed and regurgitated. This doesn't make them sparkle any less brightly. On the contrary, it means that you and I have a chance at re-creating such verbal triumphs. Spontaneity is entirely in the ear of the beholder.

Our Elemental Breakdown

To explore wit by examining witty sayings is like studying a snowflake by putting it under the microscope. By the time you're ready to look at the intricate structure in your well-heated lab, all you'll see is a little puddle of water. Far better to examine the process by which snowflakes are made, which brings us to the elements of wit.

First, we examine where wit comes from. In order to amusingly combine concepts on the fly, you're going to need some concepts. And so we begin with **Hustle**, meaning the way you'll acquire these ideas. The word doesn't generally refer to library research, and that's why it fits: Most of the concepts the Wits used were absorbed from the popular culture of everyday life. There are books of quotations, newspaper columns, things hollered by angry spouses, movie lines and more. The best spontaneity, we shall see, is well practiced.

Then comes **Flow**, a somewhat magical concept that explains how you let your mind and mouth go. There's a whole genre of art dedicated to this: Rap. How musical improvisation happens is key to the practice of wit.

Closely related is **Intuition**, which is basically a way to describe the thinking we do when we're not thinking. It often seems that the best ideas bubble up from some hidden part of the brain, and it's vital to figure out how much you trust those ideas before you open your mouth and voice them.

You'll want to have **Confidence**. Since there's not much call for slow wit, you need to be ready with a quip and just as ready to recover if it doesn't fly. Insecurity is inadmissible; the best insurance is self-assurance.

And the most time-tested way to lessen inhibitions comes via **Refreshment**, our only slightly euphemistic description of those substances that flow freely at cocktail parties and loosen tongues. This chapter should not be read by children or pregnant women.

These are our conditions for wit. From there, we move on to its purpose.

The Bible and biology agree that our primary job as humans is to propagate the species, so we must highlight wit's role in **Romance**. Seduction via repartee is the goal of a thousand sonnets, and a fairly evolutionarily sound one at that: The suitor who can entrance his (or her!) beloved on the fly will probably also be able to improvise ways to protect that future mate from saber-toothed tigers.

Similarly, the element of **Charm** is key to social advancement in all human societies. If romance is wit directed at one lucky person, charm is a more diffuse sharing of wit with the world.

And should that wit be coupled with ideas on improving society, you have **Righteousness**. Brilliant ideas need to be delivered brilliantly and wit will convince people to listen.

Then there are the specific life events that call for wit, some obviously and some less so.

The basic human quality of **Resilience** is how we move forward. When our plans crumble in our hands, we need spontaneous creativity to create new ones.

In everyday **Conversation**, wit is the salt on the meal, the attribute that makes us want to keep discussing weighty matters.

Wit can be used to cruel ends, but it can just as easily be comprised of **Compassion**. The two are sides of a coin. We will choose to have it land with the smiling face up.

And finally, in this age of Twitter, the need for **Brevity** has never been more apparent. Here more than ever, succinct phrasing is the whole point.

A Note on Methods

E. B. White observed that dissecting a joke is like dissecting a frog: No one laughs and the frog dies. On the other hand, a collection of aphorisms can, in the words of aphoristologist James Geary, "fit easily into the overhead compartment of your brain and contain everything you need to get through a rough day at the office or a dark night of the soul." This book intends to stuff your overhead compartment full of lively frogs. As such, we'll keep things moving along at a steady clip and sock all the references and further reading in the back.

On occasion, we will have to retell famous quips, but we will do with the understanding that, as *New Yorker* television critic Emily Nussbaum wrote, "there's nothing more numbingly Soviet than summarizing comedy."

Many of the best witticisms are so famous they don't need repeating, so in those cases we'll look at the context: How exactly did Churchill have that line about being sober in the morning ready so quickly? (Hint: By stealing it.)

And you'll find quizzes, checklists and illustrations throughout, all to ensure that the next time you're in an awkward situation, you'll have kept these wits about you.

ONE

Hustle

◆ ◆ ◆

Can you try to be a wit? The answer is a definite yes. Will your efforts come to anything? The answer is decidedly less certain. The Inverse Law of Repartee has it that the harder an individual attempts to be funny in social situations, the stronger the stink of flop sweat that wafts off that poor soul. Effort and effervescence simply can't share the same room: It takes hard work to get those bubbles in the Champagne but you don't want to think about that when you're popping a bottle.

This is perhaps best illustrated by Ricky Gervais as David Brent in the very first episode of the original U.K. version of *The Office*. As the boss who's also a "chilled-out entertainer" shows a new hire around the workplace, he repeatedly stresses how hilarious he is. The Brentmaster General is put to the test when his employee Tim jokingly explains why he has encased his gawky deskmate's stapler in jelly.

"Gareth, it's only a trifling matter," Tim mumbles.

Brent sputters with laughter.

"Here we go!" he chortles as he high-fives Tim. "Always like this!"

"You should probably put him in custardy," the new hire offers.

"Ha, he's gonna fit in here!" narrates Brent unnecessarily. "We're like Vic and Bob," he says, pointing to Tim and himself in a reference to a British comedy duo, "and one extra one. Oh God!"

"Yeah, I'm more worried, really, about damage to company property, that's all," says Gareth.

There's a long pause and a look of strain on Brent's face. "I'm just trying," he says under his breath. "I'm just trying to think of other desserts," he says.

He does not.

There is another pause to ensure the audience has time to cringe. (This pause lasts forever, and is essentially the gestation period of Ricky Gervais's career. By the time it ends, he's a comedy legend.)

Effort has killed wit, and it wasn't even close. The old Thomas Edison bit about genius being 99 percent perspiration and 1 percent inspiration would appear to be accurate in the ingredients but not the end result: The overwhelming amount of exertion drowns out anything clever and the recipe produces desperation.

But it feels antiquated and elitist to say that true wits are born that way and the rest of us should simply try not to crowd them at cocktail parties, if we're even invited. Surely in this, the age of the meritocracy, hard work and determination count for something.

There's no time like the present to start preparing.

Here let us pause to quote *The Simpsons*:

LENNY: Wow, I've never seen you have so many lunch beers before, Homer!

CARL: I concur! (*They stare at this unexpected eloquence.*) Word-of-the-day calendar. (*He holds up an entry for "conquer."*)

So let's say yes, effort can make you witty—provided it's deployed correctly and well in advance. Just as no amount of strain and head scratching will help you in the middle of an exam you haven't studied for, there's no sense racking the old brain for a comeback that isn't there. And as you never know when you'll need a clever retort, there's no time like the present to start preparing. But how? You can begin by acting like an annoying bird.

The Magpie Mind

The magpie is perhaps the perfect mascot for wit. It is reputed to be one of the most intelligent of all animals, one of the only birds capable of recognizing its own reflection in the mirror and grieving for lost comrades. Less impressively, the word "magpie" is used to describe someone who chatters noisily. And more to the point, it can describe someone who collects indiscriminately, the sort of person who in an extreme case would be featured on a hoarding reality show.

This sort of collecting is where wit must begin, and we can look to the beginning of a Great Wit's career to see the magpie mind at work. Tom Stoppard, the English playwright and inveterate improver of Hollywood screenplays, began his literary career with the 1966 novel *Lord Malquist & Mr. Moon*. In a 2005 reissue, Stoppard used a new introduction to shed some light on his early creative process.

"Almost every random page brings back a memory of magpie pickings from (mostly) other people," he wrote. "Who would guess (as I instantly remembered) that when Malquist speaks of the mourning of (the unnamed) Churchill being 'imposed upon a sentimental people,' I was consciously recalling a favorite and far superior sentence in A. J. Liebling's account of an English boxer years earlier: 'a fat man whose gift for public suffering endeared him to a sentimental people'? My trick mind still retrieves such shiny objects intact even though I can never remember my mobile phone number."

Obviously it helps to have such a mind—more on that to come—but it's just as important to know what you're stockpiling. The shiny things in the world of language are felicitous turns of phrase, bits of wisdom well expressed, or simply ideas worth setting aside for later.

Among other things, Winston Churchill was one of the master magpies of the twentieth century, and he started assembling his hoard very early. Like all Victorian schoolboys, young Winston's education featured a fair chunk of rote memorization. The great statesman embraced and recommended this, perhaps most overtly in his memoir *My Early Life: 1874–1904*:

"It is a good thing for an uneducated man to read books of quotations. *Bartlett's Familiar Quotations* is an admirable work, and I studied it intently. The quotations when engraved upon the memory give you good thoughts."

And so it is no surprise that, in the thrust and parry of debate, parliamentary or otherwise, Churchill could draw on an extensive catalogue of good thoughts. This mental engraving was an effort, one he worked at all his life and one of the earliest signs of the tenacity for which he became famous. His magpie mind drew from books, film, media and anywhere else he read, heard or saw a line worth repeating.

One common repository for such lines in his era was the joke column, then a staple of the popular press. Collections of one-liners abounded in newspapers of the time, which in many ways served the function Twitter does today. These columns were often American in origin—with names like "Yankee Snacks" and "Stars and Stripes"—and even more often filled with groaners, but the sheer number of them ensured some gems among the dross. A widely read man, as Churchill most certainly was, would see them all the time.

These columns generally ran without attribution, so one was free to borrow as required. On the occasions Churchill was pressed to attribute his good thoughts, he would do so. Of course, upon hearing a well-turned phrase, how often do you demand to know its provenance? Answering effervescence with pedantry isn't much fun. The more the status of the phrase turner grows, the more likely this verification is left to the historians. And as he was continually squirreling away ever more repartee in his mental filing cabinet, Churchill likely knew he would be forgiven for mixing up the credits. Some of the attributions Churchill is on record as giving include: A "witty Irishman" (that narrows it down), "As someone said . . . ," "As the cynic has said . . . ," "No, I didn't say it; but I'm sorry I didn't, because it was quite witty . . . and so true!" and "I never said it, but I wish I had."

Historians have argued that Churchill just assumed his well-read audiences would get his references, which may well be true, but it's more fun to paraphrase the title of Austin Kleon's 2012 creativity manual: He was stealing like an artist. "All creative work builds on what came before," Kleon repeats. "Nothing is completely original."

Winston Churchill wasn't being duplicitous, but he certainly was working at wit. The determined spirit who would fight them in the fields and in the streets was just making sure he had the verbal arsenal ready to go.

Magpie vs. Parrot

Stuffing your brain with funny lines and repeating them when prompted is, we can all agree, not wit. It's more likely to remind you of the groups of teenage boys who would sit in one corner of the high school cafeteria spouting dialogue at each other. Depending on when you were sitting in said cafeteria, those lines were either from *Monty Python's Flying Circus* or *The Simpsons*. And the net effect was perfectly encapsulated in the October 11, 2000, column in the *Onion* headlined "Maybe I Can Impress Her with My *Holy Grail* Quotes."

These are the limitations of quotations, and they are a bit sad. Here you have people who have taken the first step to wit. They have identified something truly clever in the world. So far, so good. They too wish to be clever. Who doesn't? So they repeat the clever thing, and it all falls apart.

This is the behavior of a parrot, not a magpie. It's just repetition, which may earn Polly a cracker but not much more. That said, the work required to take an expansive knowledge of clever culture and ably deploy it need not be onerous.

Churchill assimilated vast tracts of epigrams and aphorisms, but in many cases he twisted them just enough to grant them immortality. And naturally, timing is everything.

Thus we have "a sheep in sheep's clothing," Churchill's dismissal of Clement Attlee. "When asked, Churchill said this was based on a more pointed remark he'd once made about someone else," Ralph Keyes writes in *The Quote Verifier*, before he sources it to a newspaper joke column and thus an unknown aphorist.

And when Labour MP Bessie Braddock said, "Winston, you are drunk, and what's more you are disgustingly drunk," and he replied, "Bessie my dear, you are ugly, and what's more you are disgustingly ugly. But tomorrow I shall be sober and you shall still be disgustingly ugly," he was paraphrasing (and improving upon) W. C. Fields in the 1934 movie *It's a Gift*. In that film, the scold was crazy and would be for the rest of his life.

When Nancy Astor said, "If I were married to you, I'd put poison in your coffee," and Churchill replied, "If I were married to you, I'd drink it," he was using a line that dates back to a joke column in the *Chicago Tribune*.

And fittingly, "I am just preparing my impromptu remarks" is a line often attributed to Churchill but never verified. More probably, it's a paraphrase of Churchill's good friend Lord Birkenhead, who declared, "Winston has spent the best years of his life writing impromptu speeches." That only sounds insulting if you view wit as something unlearnable, which Churchill clearly did not.

Digesting the Jests

Winston Churchill's extensive reading of quotations was part of a wider and deeper study of the language, one he also describes with characteristic self-effacement in *My Early Life*. There he writes that he was considered such a mediocre student that he wasn't pushed to the heights of Latin and Greek; the English language was deemed the most he could manage. Over and over again, he diagrammed and color-coded sentences until he had a bone-deep knowledge of "the essential structure of the ordinary British sentence—which is a noble thing."

This sort of education is common in the biographies of many Great Wits. As a girl, Dorothy Parker attended a boarding school that put a premium on public speaking. "Each student was many times required to recite before the entire school; each girl's voice was placed," John Keats writes in his biography of Parker. "Much of the material recited was poetry, for to explore the deeps of meaning in a poem's compressed imagery demands a singularly thoughtful control of body, face, and voice, not to mention a perceptive knowledge of the poem's meanings."

Parker went on to work for *Vogue*, where her job writing captions for illustrations was menial but doubtless good preparation for the lifetime of conversations that followed. "Brevity is the soul of lingerie—as the petticoat said to the chemise" was one of her early caption successes, as was "This little pink dress will win you a beau."

They learned the good stuff, but then they also learned what to do with it. Any form of practice has to include both parts of that equation.

But let's be honest: When that cafeteria quoter of Monty Python is turned down for a date, he's not going to pick up the first volume of Winston Churchill's memoirs for consolation. He's headed online.

"How can I learn to be scathingly witty?" he might ask. "Most of the people in my life are bright intellectuals with sharp tongues. I wish to compete with them in repartee."

This is an actual question submitted by a user to Ask Metafilter back in 2007, the question-and-answer department of the popular community weblog, and the hive mind's discussion usefully sorts through the limits and possibilities of working hard at wit.

One common suggestion was to memorize quips and lines from clever TV shows and movies, but that technique obviously has its limitations.

"I have a habit of watching the reruns of my favorite TV shows over and over (and over) again," one user proudly admitted. "As a result, a lot of the quips and jokes have stuck with me, and surprisingly, I've been in real-life situations where the dialogue has inadvertently 'set up' one of those TV jokes. For example, I was in a business meeting once, and one exec happened to say, 'Can I ask a stupid question?' Before I could stop myself, I responded, 'Better than anyone I know.' (A *Golden Girls* quote, BTW)."

This is skillful parroting, but it's still parroting. As another user gently pointed out: "I would also suggest that the wittiest people concentrate on the conversation at hand rather than trying to crowbar in rehearsed bon mots."

Many recommended reading the classics, an ambiguous category of great thinkers that here ranges from the Ionian school to Steven Wright. Learning the roots of language helps, as a third points out, though a fourth chides, "[T]here is a huge difference between making clever comments on a message board and being witty in face-to-face conversations. All the research in the world is not going to make you witty, it's just going to make you well read." Which is true enough.

Eventually, shards of the argument made on these pages begin to appear. "Whatever you do, don't fall into the trap of equating wit with sarcasm, putdowns and general meanness," says a sixth. "Learn to look at life sideways instead."

And that vantage point, cleared of snark, allows this group to sketch out something approximating the traditional Enlightenment definition of wit.

"Remember that funny folk often do pretty simple tricks to make the funny on the fly," writes our final Metafilterer. "They might, for instance, put two simple but incongruous ideas together, find a way to shift the direction of a story 180 degrees from the expected direction. They might take a situation or character from an earlier conversational topic and insert it into a later part of the conversation. Now everyone has the background to understand the joke but no one, you hope, expects this combination now. You catch them off guard and they laugh, maybe."

In 2013, a version of the same question was asked again, likely by the next generation Monty Python quoter, one who has moved onto Reddit. (Message-board culture may change, but the big issues in life stay the same.) The answer voted the best was pretty much in keeping with the previous dialogue.

"The key is to become good at observation and develop a nice descriptive vocabulary," wrote this Redditor. "The balance is in finding remarks that are clever, yet not so esoteric that they fly over people's heads." Other users recommended picking random words out of the dictionary and attempting to figure out what they have in common (though that frankly seems like better prep for the SATs than an actual human conversation) and to lay off the marijuana (probably good advice on many levels).

And then there was the recommendation to "Seriously, watch *Monty Python's Flying Circus*! Watch every episode. I think about 90% of all the humor and dialogue is just pure wit." And nothing against Cleese, Palin et al., but that's how our hypothetical wit seeker found himself in this situation in the first place.

Do's and Don'ts

So we know the greats practiced and we have a rough idea of what we want to achieve, but what are the concrete lessons from all of the above? Obviously, this is the sort of ambiguous situation best addressed by a prescriptive binary checklist.

DON'T visibly rack your mind in a social situation. If it comes easily, it will be there. If it doesn't, let it go.

DON'T fight to have the last word. If it looks like work, it's not working.

DON'T credit your sources, if you can get away with it. This is the virtue of conversation over say, cough, a book. No one's going to ask to see your references, and if they do they might not be impressed by your *Golden Girls* citation.

> *Read widely, but also deeply.*

DO pay close attention to the conversation. A reference to something that's just been said is much better than one to anything else. The former indicates you're invested in the present; the latter suggests your brain is elsewhere.

DO allow your witty reputation to precede you. There's no need to remind your audience of your verbal facility, lest you come off as someone who talks too much.

DO read widely, but also deeply. Retention is key, not just of quips but the animating ideas behind them. And by reading, we'll include watching films, television and the occasional viral video. Cultural literacy and fluency is the goal.

Where to begin this list of witty media? Right here! As in: Start by finishing this book. But also as in: Throughout the book we'll be looking at witty lives for guidance, so here's a list of the works that made these wits worthy of our study. At the very least, they're guaranteed to be much more entertaining uses of your time than picking random words out of the dictionary or, with apologies to Sir Winston, reading a book of quotations.

WIT AT WORK: A CORE CURRICULUM

Benchley, Robert. The essay "Why We Laugh—or Do We?" originally published in the *New Yorker* on January 2, 1937, finds the humor in humorless studies of humor and is a perfect introduction to his style of educated nonsense.

Brand, Russell. The pinnacle of eloquent rudeness. Ease in with *Get Him to the Greek* (2010), as it's easier to understand what he's all about if you assume he's a rock star.

Collins, Gail. The best of the current crop of *New York Times* op-ed columnists, by a long shot. If you know that Mitt Romney once strapped his dog Seamus's carrier to the roof of the car during a family road trip, it's likely thanks to her. More regularly, she cleverly twists the dullest political stories into crackerjack columns.

C.K., Louis. The "Of Course, but Maybe" bit from his 2012 stand-up special *Oh My God* sums up the uneasy mix of morality and sloth that makes him both a comic's comic and an everyman's comic—in other words, everyone's comic.

Ephron, Nora. Before the self-proclaimed wallflower at the orgy felt bad about her neck, she was one of the first women in a man's world. Marvel that "A Few Words about Breasts" was published in a men's magazine, and try to read the entries under "Parker, Dorothy" before you get to "Dorothy Parker," her essay about how all idols are false.

Fey, Tina. The references and callbacks in *30 Rock* illustrate a total mastery of the internal reference. Or to put it another way, "Blergh!" is funnier the fifth time than the first.

Hitchens, Christopher. His memoir *Hitch-22*, specifically the chapter that explains the title, and why he was unapologetic about pretty much everything.

Lebowitz, Fran. This one's easy: Her one book, *The Fran Lebowitz Reader.* A magazine columnist's unimpressed view of the 1970s that dates surprisingly well.

Martin, Steve. In *The Jerk* (1979), we can see some of his breakthrough humor theory: The idea that a joke without a punch line is the funniest joke of all. Also, the improvised moment in which Martin's character Navin Johnson is hitchhiking and a truck driver stops and asks, "St. Louis?" to which he replies, "No, Navin Johnson!"

Marx, Groucho. Duck Soup. The best of vaudeville preserved on film.

Nash, Ogden. Read his animal poems, ideally aloud to small children.

Parker, Dorothy. The poems "Love Song," "Résumé" and "Interview," and then, to cheer up just a bit, "The Waltz."

Poehler, Amy. As a founding member of the Upright Citizens Brigade, she helped create modern improv. With Tina Fey, she saved both *Saturday Night Live*'s "Weekend Update" and the Golden Globes.

Stoppard, Tom. High schoolers read *Rosencrantz and Guildenstern,* and *Arcadia* may be his best work, but the shredding of the fourth wall in *The Real Inspector Hound* makes it his wittiest.

West, Kanye. Though just about all of his songs have dazzling wordplay in service of an enormous ego, "Jesus Walks" is crass evangelism at its best.

West, Mae. *She Done Him Wrong* (1933), the film that gave her the chance to use the line "when women go wrong, men go right after," and a dozen more like it.

Wilde, Oscar. *The Importance of Being Earnest* is perhaps the greatest play outside of Shakespeare. Inside Shakespeare and with apologies to Marx, it's too dark to see what's happening on stage.

{ QUIP QUIZ }

1. "I can well understand the Honourable Member's wishing to speak on. He needs the _____ badly."

   —Winston Churchill

2. "For years a secret shame destroyed my peace—
   I'd not read Eliot, Auden or MacNeice.
   But now I think a thought that brings me _____
   Neither had Chaucer, Shakespeare, Milton, Pope."

   —Justin Richardson's "Take Heart, Illiterates: An Epigram"

3. "The fake profundities of dead politicians, the treacly outpourings of fifth-rate poets, the moonlit nonsense of minor essayists—this _____ makes up the bulk of most quotation books." **—Robertson Davies**

4. "You can pretend to be _____, but you can't

pretend to be witty."   —Sacha Guitry

5. "A widely-read man never quotes _____, for the

rather obvious reason that he has read too widely."

—Hesketh Pearson

Practice	Hope	Junk	Serious	Accurately

HUSTLE WIT LIST

- ☐ DON'T Be a tryhard
- ☐ But try, hard
- ☐ Absorb smart things...
- ☐ and regurgitate them in non-gross fashion when appropriate
- ☐ Never quote Monty Python
- ☐ Really. Never

TWO

Flow

Featuring: A floppy velvet hat, the Americanization of rock climbing, Eminem, Scottish quarrelling, Jay-Z driving around Manhattan by himself while blasting Aerosmith and just the right amount of neurobiology

◆ ◆ ◆

In the early 1970s, thirty-one high-achieving art students at the University of Chicago successfully pursued and captured happiness. Fortunately they were being studied by psychologists at the time, so we know how they did it and can re-create their experience in the comfort of the present day.

First, you'll want to be a high-achieving art student. You'll ideally have won a scholarship or two, exhibited your work in galleries and hopefully have a few prizes to your name. If this is not possible, please identify some form of creative exertion you enjoy.

Second, find a room with two tables. On the first table, lay out a variety of objects. The original art students used twenty-seven, but you can probably get away with a dozen. Some recommended objects include: A floppy velvet hat, a polished gearshift, a bunch of grapes, an antique book and a small human figure.

Select a few of these objects to make a composition on Table No. 2.

Third, in the medium of your choosing, create a portrait of your assemblage. The art students used dry media like charcoal and pencil but if drawing isn't your thing, feel free to use paint, song or gesture. Take as much time as you need; we'll wait.

Finished? Well done. Now we can evaluate your performance. In the original study this was done by a team of scientists who took notes and photographs throughout the exercise, as well as a panel of five well-known artists who rated the finished products, but here you're encouraged to grade yourself based on your answers to the following questions:

How many of the objects did you touch before choosing the ones you'd draw/paint/dance around? The more, the better. Jot this number down, then divide it by five.

How intently did you examine the objects? Rate yourself on a scale of one to five, with one being "Not much" and five being "I tried on the floppy velvet hat, observed my reflection in the polished gearshift, ate a grape and knew then that these objects simply had to be drawn/painted/danced around."

Now let's look at your drawing/poem/interpretive dance. Did you create it without interruption, or did you frequently pause to change media, adjust the hat or simply take stock of the challenge? Give yourself one point just for showing up, then add a point for each moment of pause and reflection, to a maximum of five.

Finally, how much did you alter reality in your artwork? Give yourself one point if you basically copied the arrangement, and an additional point for each creative flourish you added. If you painted the floppy velvet hat on the head of a Komodo dragon, give yourself a full five points.

Now total your score. As you may have guessed, that number, out of twenty, is a measure of how much effort you put into this little assignment. If you zipped through in a quick and efficient manner, you likely got an F. And the real injustice is that you failed precisely because you're a problem solver. In this bizarro world experiment, the high scorers are the problem finders. If you deliberated at every step and introduced new challenges where there were none, you probably did pretty well.

In the real-life study on which this little exercise is based, those scores were then compared to professional assessments of the finished works. The more challenging the students made the assignment, the more original the resulting artwork. And almost as a side finding, the artist judges unwittingly correlated originality almost perfectly to overall aesthetic value. The original *are* the best, at least by the standards of the art world.

And furthermore, the researchers followed as many of the students as they could through their careers, and generally found the problem-making originals to be more successful than the problem solvers.

They Just Called It Flow

So what, if anything, do these portraits of hats and gearshifts have to do with happiness? Or, especially, wit? Or, even more specifically, Jay-Z? Absolutely nothing. It's a classic case of misdirection, a magic trick in which a larger movement conceals a smaller, more vital one. Or, more scientifically, it's like the observer effect: If we actually said what was being studied, we would have altered the outcome before we began.

But it was a necessary part of the process, as it was in 1970 when Mihaly Csikszentmihalyi (him again) and J. W. Getzels ran through more refined versions of the above experiment to produce the paper "Discovery-Oriented Behavior and the Originality of Creative Products." Getzels, a professor at the University of Chicago who died in 2001, spent his career studying creativity, intelligence and the difference between the two. In studies like this one, he found that the most creative students were the problem finders, while those with the highest IQs were the problem solvers.

Cheeks Sent Me High

Csikszentmihalyi (pronounced, it must be said, cheeks-sent-me-high) was Getzels's protégé, and studies like this one sent him in a markedly different direction. He continued to work on creativity and education, but he became most interested in the process, not the product. When we say the most successful students were finding problems, what exactly do we mean? Who in their right mind would want to be part of the problem? And that was it: They weren't in their right minds, but rather something better.

In addition to these artists, rock climbers enjoy being part of the problem. In 1969, Csikszentmihalyi had written a piece for the University of Chicago magazine headlined "The Americanization of Rock Climbing." On its craggy surface, it had little to do with education or creativity. The thesis was simple: The sport of mountaineering, in its European origins, was focused on the crisp Alpine air and beautiful views. The modern American version called it rock climbing and was much more focused on efficiently scaling peaks with the best methods and technology. With perhaps a tinge of sadness, the Italian-born and European-raised Csikszentmihalyi concluded, "A game activity which until a generation ago was performed leisurely, within a complex logico-meaningful framework of experiences is now becoming a calculated, precise, expert enterprise within a much narrower framework of experiences."

By 1974, Csikszentmihalyi had begun to probe the links between his artists and his rock climbers. This was when he coined the term that has defined him to this day: Autotelic experience! Well, no. The term "autotelic" means "self-goal," thus defining an experience that's pleasurable in and of itself. But this isn't what the rock climbers, dancers, composers and chess masters called their mental states. They just called it *flow*.

Losing Yourself (in a Good Way)

With this concept, Csikszentmihalyi became one of the founders of the positive psychology movement. It took a few decades, but eventually scientists like Martin Seligman and Ed Diener began to work the word "happiness" into academic research, and soon the scientific pursuit of the H-word became the gigantic industry it is today.

And flow is an integral part of happiness. When you're not thinking about that email you need to return, or counting the minutes until you can justify a coffee break, or rushing to finish one task so you can start the next; when you're so deep into an activity, be it intense concentration or effortless conversation, that time has stopped and you are floating along in a pleasure-filled bubble, you're in flow and, while you'd never stop to ask "Am I happy right now?" the obvious answer is yes.

As Csikszentmihalyi later explained in the introduction to one of his many books on the subject, "The term [flow] had been introduced as a metaphor by some respondents to describe their feelings while involved in their favorite activities, and the short Anglo-Saxon word seemed preferable to the more clumsy, if more precise, term, autotelic experience."

Of course, the word "flow" had been widely used before these studies, to describe rivers and streams, electrical current and menstruation. And while Csikszentmihalyi's artists and athletes all hit upon the term while searching for a way to describe their mental states, there is a group of artists who use the word "flow" without prompting. We call these artists rappers.

"Rappers have a word for what they do when the rhythm sparks them; they call it *flow*," writes Adam Bradley in *Book of Rhymes: The Poetics of Hip Hop*. "In a compelling twist of etymology, the word rhythm is derived from the Greek *rheo*, meaning flow. Flow is where poetry and music communicate in a common language of rhythm."

"The purpose in life is not to find yourself. It's to lose yourself."

And though they may not know it, the rappers and the psychologists are really talking about the same thing. The word is used organically in both cases: The participants racked their brains to describe what they were doing, and everyone came back with "flow." And consider what flow, in the psychological sense, has evolved to mean. In his columns and commencement speeches, David Brooks has distilled the research as follows:

The purpose in life is not to find yourself. It's to lose yourself.

Those last two words should sound familiar even to those with only a passing knowledge of rap, as they are the title of one of Eminem's biggest hits, the Academy Award–winning song at the center of the 2002 autobiographical film *8 Mile*.

As the hook for that song goes:

"You better lose yourself in the music, the moment
You own it, you better never let it go."

The movie, and indeed Eminem's rapping life, centers around ciphers, the rap battles in which competitors joust with impromptu rhymes and insults. They need to have flow, in the rap sense, but also in the psychological sense. Csikszentmihalyi describes what all flow activities have in common. Here's his description from the book *Flow*, spliced through with lyrics from "Lose Yourself."

> *It provided a sense of discovery, a creative feeling of transporting the person to a new reality ("Snap back to reality, Oh there goes gravity"). It pushed the person to higher levels of performance ("Make me king, as we move toward a new world order"), and led to previously undreamed-of states of consciousness ("A normal life is boring, but superstardom's close to post mortem"). In short, it transformed the self by making it more complex.*

The cipher is "a competitive and collaborative space created when MCs gather to exchange verses, either in freestyle battles or in collaborative lyrical brainstorming sessions," Bradley writes. "The cipher is a verbal cutting contest that prizes wit and wordplay above all else." Of course, Eminem didn't invent the cipher. The practice of "playing the dozens" is long-standing in black American culture, and there are variants in just about every language ever spoken.

One particularly similar ancestor is the art of flyting, an old Scottish word that means quarrelling or contention. The oldest Caledonian example is a sixteenth-century exchange called "The Flyting of Dunbar and Kennedy," and it is essentially two poets calling each other the most despicable things they can imagine to win the favor of the king. You're short, you're ugly, you can't rhyme, you're a cuckold, washerwomen take in their laundry when they see you coming, fishwives throw things at you, your ancestors were a she-bear and a devil, you once defecated so much at sea that you nearly sank your boat: That sort of thing. All of this is a handy rejoinder to those who complain about the crassness of modern rap.

(On that crassness, for a moment: It's undeniably there, but far too often used to dismiss the genre outright. Take the complexity of Lil Wayne, a rapper whose many tattoos and addiction to cough syrup may disguise the fact that he's probably really good at cryptic crosswords, and specifically this line, for which all you need to know is that "G" is short for "gangster": "Real Gs move in silence like lasagna." Even musical greats like ?uestlove didn't get it at first, tweeting the line with the hashtag #AmIGettinOld? The key, as per the Talmudic site RapGenius.com, is that the letter "g" is silent in the word "lasagna," though it also notes a reference to a Notorious B.I.G. line about criminals moving in "silence and violence.")

To be immersed in this sort of competitive rhyming is to both have flow and be in flow. Whether the deployed rhymes are memorized or ad-libbed is a source of some debate, but there's no doubt it should sound impromptu. It is perhaps the most direct way we produce wit, cutting phrases that have more than enough immediacy to make up for their lack of polish. It is also a reminder that wit is the opposite of ironic detachment; true wit requires total engagement. And the master of the format, the self-proclaimed greatest rapper to ever walk the earth, is of course Jay-Z.

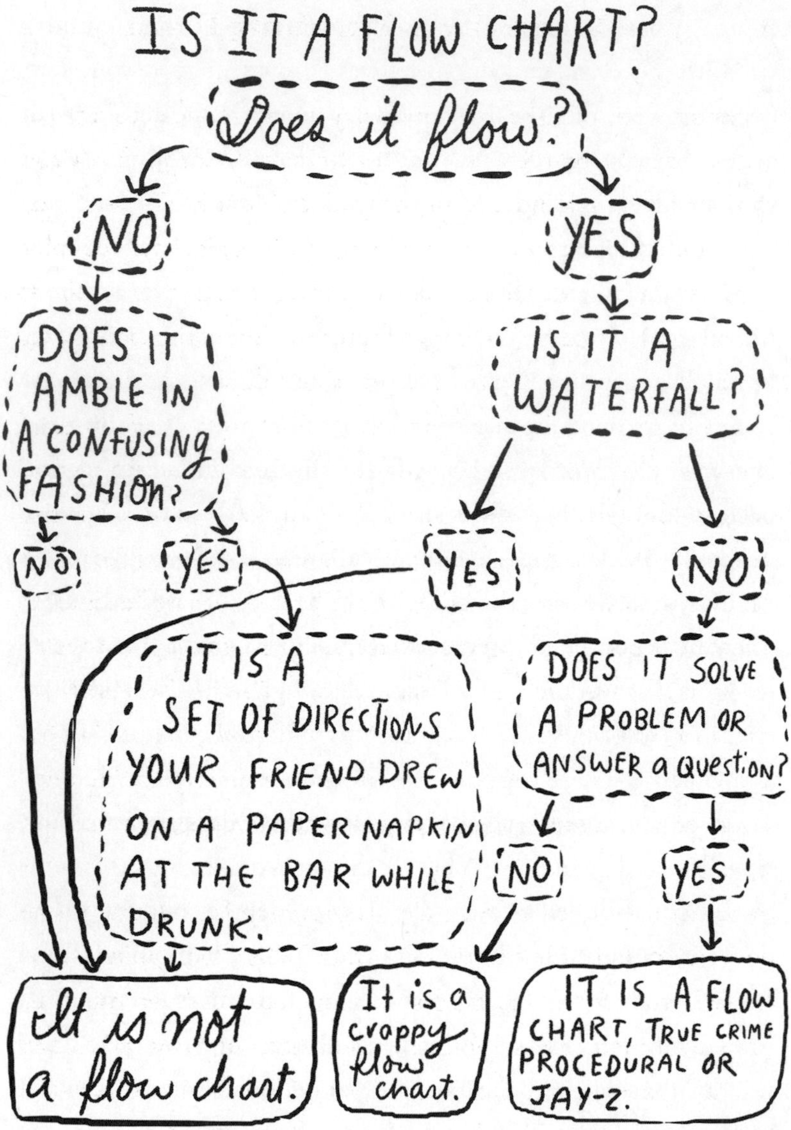
IS IT A FLOW CHART?
Does it flow?
NO
YES
DOES IT AMBLE IN A CONFUSING FASHION?
IS IT A WATERFALL?
NO
YES
YES
NO
IT IS A SET OF DIRECTIONS YOUR FRIEND DREW ON A PAPER NAPKIN AT THE BAR WHILE DRUNK.
DOES IT SOLVE A PROBLEM OR ANSWER a QUESTION?
NO
YES
It is not a flow chart.
It is a crappy flow chart.
IT IS A FLOW CHART, TRUE CRIME PROCEDURAL OR JAY-Z.

He Doesn't Write Anything Down

In the summer of 1978, Shawn Carter was introduced to rap. As he tells it in the first line of his 2010 memoir, *Decoded*, "I saw the circle before I saw the kid in the middle." The kid's name was Slate and he was rhyming, "throwing out couplet after couplet like he was in a trance, for a crazy long time." Carter was inspired. "That night, I started writing rhymes in my spiral notebook. From the beginning it was easy, a constant flow."

In one form or another, that flow made him Jay-Z: Winner of more than a dozen Grammys, part-owner of an NBA team, multi-millionaire, Mr. Beyoncé, former crack dealer who now has the ears of presidents and CEOs. And as he famously sang, he's "not a businessman—I'm a business, man." Yes, he has perseverance, savvy and acumen, all of which have built his personal fortune to an estimated half billion dollars. It should also be noted that he stabbed a bootlegging record producer in the stomach and shot his strung-out brother in the arm, so there's a certain bloody minded-ness at play, too. But his ascent began with wit, expressed through flow.

"The thing is, there are no clouds above Jay. He is hands down the wittiest person I've ever met," wrote Dream Hampton in *Vibe* magazine in 1998. "He misses nothing and will floor you with quick one-liners. He is, more often than not, laughing. His laugh is odd, like a sneeze, and just as contagious. He drives around Manhattan by himself, blasting Aerosmith. And if for some reason you missed your daily fix of *The Simpsons* or *Seinfeld*, you can call Jay and he will act out the episode for you."

His actual process of rapping is fascinating, mainly because those who see it in action are generally floored by it. As a savvy promoter, Carter knows this and burnishes the legend.

In the early 1990s, as Zach O'Malley Greenburg recounts in his business-of-Jay-Z book, *Empire State of Mind*, a new, rap-savvy talent scout at Atlantic Records was trying to sign Jay. The label set him up in a recording studio at some expense, and one of the producers was nervous to find their chosen one had nothing written down for his big chance.

"We've been here for three hours, and they've just been laughing and talking about stuff and haven't been talking about music. So I finally was like, 'Jay, come on man, you gotta fucking lay your vocals, man. This is on my ass, I'm wasting studio time, I'm almost over budget!'" Patrick "A Kid Called Roots" Lawrence told the author.

At which point Jay picked up a notebook, made some scribbling gestures, paced around the room muttering and went into the recording booth. The pad, Lawrence recalls, was empty; the writing had been a charade. "He was doing it as a fucking joke, like just to show people," Lawrence told O'Malley Greenburg. "That was when I was like, 'This guy is the best rapper.'"

As he moved up in the music world, this story happened time and time again. In the 2004 documentary *Fade to Black*, Jay-Z is in the studio with superproducer Rick Rubin and Mike D of the Beastie Boys, two men with considerably more experience than A Kid Called Roots.

"Just to see the way he writes, I've never seen anything like it," Rubin says. "Because he doesn't write anything down."

"Yeah, he just does it all in here," Mike D replies, finger to cranium.

"Yeah, he just kinda sits there, listens to the track, writes a verse and then goes and does it."

In anecdote after anecdote, this is repeated: Jay-Z walks in cold, mumbles a bit to himself, then enters the recording booth to produce a flawless rhyme. How *does* he do it, exactly?

That's what radio host and hip-hop historian Dave "Davey D" Cook tried to figure out when Jay and his entourage visited his show in the late 1990s.

"While folks hovered around Jay-Z, I pulled [fellow rapper Memphis] Bleek to the side and asked him, 'Fam, be honest, is it true what I heard? Does Jay really go into the studio and spit complete songs off the dome?'" he recounts in his essay "The Meeting with a President and a 'King.'"

"Being a former emcee myself, I was trying hard to understand the process. Was he doing a bunch of retakes and punch-ins? Was he building upon and reworking old rhymes, a trick I used to do back in the days? Did Jay have things on paper that he would look at that would trigger a bunch of rhymes he had secretly memorized the night before?"

In other words, is Jay-Z cheating at a game of wits? These charges are similar to ones leveled at Oscar Wilde, who was known to awkwardly steer conversations toward his prewritten bon mots. Similarly, in the eighteenth-century costume-party battles of wit featured in the 1996 French film *Ridicule*, the cheating aristocrats actually did jot their impromptu lines down on the paper fans they carefully held at eye level.

Davey D is assured this is not the case. There were no paper fans or stage-managed conversations at play; instead, "many of the song concepts are constantly being worked out in Jay's head and by the time he gets to the studio, he spits flawlessly."

In a 2005 *Rolling Stone* cover story on Jay, Touré offered a more detailed explanation. "Part of why Jay can flow so well is because he's learned to write without writing. When he was out in the streets hustling he found himself coming up with great rhymes and no easy way to write them down so he learned to memorize his songs, then developed the capacity to store six or more songs in his head. When he became a recording artist he'd listen to a track ten or twenty times, then start mumbling to himself—on *Fade to Black*, the film detailing his 2003 retirement concert, he called it 'my rainman'—and in his mind the song comes into shape. Within as little as twenty minutes he'll get in the booth and spit an intricately-written rhyme."

So what can his rainman tell our rainmen? The most useful thing would be how to get into flow, and a roadmap to that state is found in his memoir *Decoded*. That's not the point of the book, a song-by-song breakdown of his oeuvre that aims to prove once and for all rap is poetry, social commentary and perhaps the art form of our time. This may be most effective for the hit "99 Problems," a song that famously follows the title with the words "but a bitch ain't one." That seems to confirm every preconception about the misogyny of rap, but as Jay-Z argues, it's really just "bait for lazy critics." The meaning of bitch changes in each verse, but it's never a woman. Most pointedly, it's a police dog in the second verse, as the narrator is having his car searched for "doing fifty-five in a fifty-four," or for no reason other than the color of his skin. But then, he does have a trunk full of drugs. And finally, as Jay-Z writes, it's the "larger presumption of guilt from the cradle that leads you to having the crack in your trunk in the first place."

What he's done here is an impressive yoking of dissimilar ideas, to quote Samuel Johnson's 1781 definition of wit, but it's how he does it that makes it universal. Just as Mihaly Csikszent-mihalyi pivoted from the art students' finished products to their creative process, here we can turn to the mental mechanics that built songs like this and, in turn, Jay-Z's career. First, there are the hours and hours—almost certainly, as per Malcolm Gladwell's overly popular popularization of Herbert Simon and William Chase's examination of elite performers, ten thousand of them accrued before the age of twenty—of vocabulary building

"I was good at battling and I practiced like a sport," Jay-Z writes. "I'd spend free time reading the dictionary, building my vocabulary for battles."

Then, before he became the writer who didn't write, he wrote. All the time. Everywhere. Again from *Decoded*: "If I was crossing a street with my friends and a rhyme came to me, I'd break out my binder, spread it on a mailbox or lamppost and write the rhyme before I crossed the street."

That was all in preparation for the ciphers, his way to practice against an opponent. With enough of that, he developed a self-confidence, the projection of which is, to use the hip-hop term, "swagger." Viewed from where he is now, the opponent was almost a straw man, a punching bag. He honed his skills in combat but the real battle was to be better than the competitor he was before, not the competitor who was before him. Then, once he entered the recording studio, he was completely at ease.

"When a track is right, I feel like it's mine from the second I hear it," he writes. "I own it." This is what Csikszentmihalyi calls the paradox of control, as the rapper could quite possibly miss the beat, flub a line or otherwise make a mistake. The fact that the challenge remains matched to his skill—that it remains a flow activity—is what keeps it exciting. Which may be why Jay-Z keeps coming out of retirement to rap again.

So the steps are reading widely, writing extensively, competing constantly and ever increasing the challenges to meet his continually honed skills. The hustler in him may rather be licensing a new line of Rocawear, but flow—both psychological and in the hip-hop sense—is its own reward. All of our Great Wits follow these steps in one way or another, but Jay-Z stands apart in that making it look easy is more than a point of pride, it's an occupational requirement.

Flow in the Brain

Could we know more about what his brain does and how it does it? Certainly, and this brings us to the third and final kind of flow. Observing the human brain at work is one of the frontiers of science, but we are very, very far from watching neurons twitch and thoughts emerge in real time. The main (and somewhat blunt) tool in this field is functional magnetic resonance imaging, or fMRI. With this expensive machinery, we can see flow—as in blood flow. The functional part means they can watch the blood coursing through your veins while you're conscious and active, though the size of the machine makes it unlikely that Mihaly Csikszent-mihalyi will be strapping it to a rock climber any time soon.

What has been done, and very recently at that, is to have freestyle rappers enter the fMRI lab and do their thing under observation. In a study published in *Scientific Reports* in November 2012, improvised and rehearsed performances by twelve male freestyle rappers were compared and contrasted. Not surprisingly, the preparatory work indicated that all subjects demonstrated a high degree of verbal fluency (above the eightieth percentile), which "highlights the importance of superior linguistic skills in this genre, which requires rapid online formulation of meaningful, rhyming words and phrases within a prescribed tempo and rhythm." (In other words, flow.)

The findings are preliminary, but they do point the way toward what a flow state looks like. The activity of interest takes place in the prefrontal cortex: The medial part of this brain area appears to be much more active during freestyling, while the dorsolateral part is subdued. What may be happening here, the researchers posit, is the parts of the brain responsible for language are working hard at "spontaneous phonetic encoding and articulation of rapidly selected words during improvisation"—harder than they do during rehearsed songs—while the parts "where information is processed prior to its gaining access to the motor system" are subdued.

This description is purposely vague, both because the neurobiology is beyond the scope of this book and because it's very early days. The researchers "propose that this dissociated pattern reflects a state in which internally motivated, stimulus-independent behaviors are allowed to unfold in the absence of conscious volitional control," which fits in nicely with everything we know about flow. But really, the results just hint at this, and there's much more work to be done.

Still, there's enough potential here for excitement. One day we might be able to design drugs that induce this freestyling state, as a way to seed the clouds for a brainstorming session. It may be that those drugs already exist in the forms of caffeine, alcohol and LSD, as there are certainly many creative people who would vouch for their positive effects. As well, if the potential to toggle back and forth between spontaneity and calculation can be harnessed, we could finally vanquish that myth about nine-tenths of our brains being underutilized. We could freestyle on cue, quickly and in any environment, losing ourselves while staying in complete control.

But until that day arrives, we can console ourselves by listening to exactly that happening in the music of Jay-Z.

{ QUIP QUIZ }

1. "I've never much enjoyed going to _____. . . . The unreality of painted people standing on a platform saying things they've said to each other for months is more than I can overlook." —John Updike

2. "In skating over thin ice, our safety is in our _____."
   —Ralph Waldo Emerson

3. "Your memory is a _____; *you* forget—*it* doesn't."

—John Irving

4. "I'm not exactly in the moment, but somewhere _____ to it."

—Jonathan Goldstein

5. "I sneezed on the beat and the beat got _____."

—Beyoncé

Plays	Speed	Monster	Adjacent	Sicker

Flow wit list

- ☐ Lose yourself (turn off GPS)
- ☐ Be as engaged as Elizabeth Taylor
- ☐ ~~Try rapping?~~
- ☐ Work at it so it comes effortlessly when you need it

THREE

Intuition

Featuring: THE TRUTH, THE DANGER OF THE BLURT,
DEL CLOSE, SIGMUND FREUD, OSCAR LEVANT, GEORGE
GERSHWIN AND STEVE MARTIN

◆ ◆ ◆

We all say the wrong thing at the wrong time every now and then. What's considerably rarer is saying the right thing at the wrong time. While the outcomes may be the same for the speaker—embarrassment, shame, a general casting out by polite society—the trick of getting the timing wrong in *just* the right way makes it much more enjoyable for the audience.

It also comes close to the definition of a Kinsley gaffe, named for the journalist Michael Kinsley's description of the occasions on which a politician inadvertently and offensively tells the truth. Politicians monopolize this blunder because there's rarely a right time for them to be perfectly candid, so when it happens this honesty usually comes at some professional cost. Sometimes this is the kind of thing captured on a microphone no one expects to be live—Jesse Jackson expressing a desire to castrate then-candidate

Barack Obama, for instance—but the more interesting cases occur when the politician knows full well he's in public and can't help himself.

We associate spontaneity with truth in a deep, hardwired way. The reasoning is so innate we rarely spell it out: A lie would take time to formulate, but if someone just blurts something, well, it must be true. This explains the use of word-association games in psychology, supposedly a window into the inner mind. The legal principle of the excited utterance works the same way: Comments made while witnessing a startling event may be admissible in court, the rationale being that the great stress keeps the declarant honest. This is, in a word, Intuition. It's what you say when you don't have time to think about what you'll say. It's also the connection between Hustle—all those erudite things you've lodged into your brain—and Flow, the state in which they come tumbling out.

And while spontaneity is a liability in some professions—no one wants to hear their lawyer riffing in front of a grand jury—it's an asset in many others. In improvisational comedy, for instance, there's no greater goal than to take down the barriers of propriety and act freely.

Yes, And?

Arguably, the most successful modern practitioners of the form were all taught by Del Close. Much of the early Second City and *Saturday Night Live* casts followed his teachings and the annual Del Close Marathon of improv in New York attracts comedians from around the world, but to the wider world he will probably be best remembered for a bit part as a droning English teacher in *Ferris Bueller's Day Off*. Together with Charna Halpern and Kim "Howard" Johnson, Close set his principles down in print in *Truth in Comedy: The Manual of Improvisation*, a book recommended by the likes of Bill Murray, John Belushi, Gilda Radner and Mike Myers.

"The subconscious is a lot smarter than most people think," the authors explain. "Very often, when a beginning improviser gets the impulse to say or do something in a scene, he ignores it. When his subconscious provides him with a sudden idea for the scene, and he doesn't understand the reason for making this 'crazy' choice, his ego considers it a mistake. The only *real* mistake here is ignoring the inner voice."

Hence the famous rule "Just say yes," or more accurately, "Yes, and . . ."

But what if listening to that inner voice *is* a mistake? What if it feeds you wonderful zingers that will ruin your career? What if your subconscious has a death wish? Here we must take a brief detour into Freudian psychology, if only because everyone uses the good doctor's terminology if not his meanings.

In *The Psychopathology of Everyday Life*, his first popular (and best-titled) book, Dr. Sigmund Freud focuses on what might lie behind the many errors, mistakes and omissions that fill our days. Did you leave that umbrella at work by mistake—or because you secretly felt compelled to return there? These parapraxes, commonly known as Freudian slips, allegedly reveal innermost desires. Of course, as a cigar is often just a cigar, we often just forget an umbrella.

Freud also wrote a whole book on wit—*Wit and Its Relation to the Unconscious*—which is unfortunately often translated to make the subject *"Jokes"* and not *"Wit."* The whole point of the book is to find the mysterious connection between jokes and wit, so declaring them synonymous is like saying the chicken is the egg: No way to order an omelette.

Freud stakes this out quite clearly when he argues that while we'd all like to make jokes, "the joke-work is not at everyone's command, and altogether only a few people have a plentiful amount of it; and these are distinguished by being spoken of as having 'wit.' 'Wit' appears in this connection as a special capacity—rather in the class of the old mental faculties; and it seems to emerge fairly independently of the others, such as intelligence, imagination, memory, etc. We must therefore presume the presence in these 'witty' people of special inherited dispositions or psychical determinants which favour the joke-work. . . . Wit shows in a most pronounced manner the character of an involuntary 'inspiration' or a sudden flash of thought."

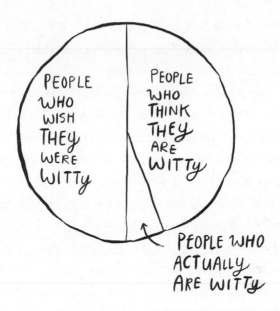

This description perfectly explains the great promise and probable disappointment of most improv comedy. In theory, the idea of a performer tossing the script aside to draw solely upon involuntary inspiration is exhilarating. In practice, well, "altogether only a few people" can pull it off.

What wit gives those lucky enough to possess it, Freud argues, is "the means of surmounting restrictions and of opening up otherwise inaccessible pleasure sources." Those sources are located in the unconscious, and this is a key point: You can consciously construct a joke, but the wit of it will arrive from the unconscious. (Freud generally preferred the word "unconscious" to "subconscious," but for our purposes they're interchangeable.)

Or as the improv manual puts it, "the ego is the part of the mind that hangs on to preconceived notions about scenes, so the best improvisers always strive to overcome their own egos. They've learned to trust their inner voices to their unconscious right choices."

They are, in other words, living by their wits. But as the old saw about the sword has it, if you live by it, you must die by it as well. The improv experts tell the students that "there is a part of the student his brain that really does know how to do this work quite well—if he would just get out of his own way!" But life is not a stage at the fringe festival, and a rampaging unconscious is the very definition of a Freudian nightmare.

And furthermore, many of the people practicing improv really have no idea what improv is. That's the contention of Matt Besser, Ian Roberts and Matt Walsh, who with Amy Poehler founded the Upright Citizens Brigade—an improv group so influential that they host the aforementioned Del Close Marathon each year—and who without Amy Poehler wrote the very technical *Upright Citizens Brigade Comedy Improvisation Manual.*

They did so, Ian Roberts explains, in part because there was a widely believed myth that "getting out of your own way" is all improv is:

> *There's no other endeavor where someone would say there's not a method to do it. Where as crazily, there are people who say, "Just get out there and be free, say the first thing that comes to mind, the first time you get on stage you can improv, and the only thing standing in your way are your inhibitions." To which I say your inhibitions result from having no technique! I mean, if you tried to drive a car with no idea how to drive, it doesn't mean the answer is to get out of your own way and just do it!*

Roberts grudgingly admits there's a role for intuition, but only once technique has been thoroughly mastered.

"Here's the thing: There's a process to get your 'intuition,' and that is not having no technique, to say the first thing that comes to your mind," he explained.

"Someone who is intuitively funny understands patterns. They understand the comic engine and how to keep being funny. If you see a good comedy scene, a good sitcom, that has a game. And the character in that game is funny consistently because he is the way he is. If the guy's this way, then when he goes to the racetrack, he does this. If he has a birthday party for his wife, he does this. *That's* what we're teaching people."

But what if you do give free rein to the unconscious? What if you don't have technique and just let your id all hang out? Could that possibly work? In that case, you very well might become Oscar Levant. Whether it worked for him is an open question.

Meet Oscar Levant

Levant was born on December 27, 1906, to Russian Jews in Pittsburgh. He took up the piano at an early age and became a close friend of George Gershwin, and later his greatest interpreter. His musical skills took him to Hollywood though it was his mordant wit that truly made him famous. His incisive putdowns of anyone and anything made him a star on *Information Please*, a radio quiz show, and led to a series of roles as a wisecracking piano player in films like *An American in Paris*. He wrote three memoirs, was regularly featured in gossip columns and had an eponymous television talk show, but his true contribution to American popular culture came in having the first modern celebrity meltdown. His prescription-drug addictions and frequent commitments to mental institutions were the stuff of late-night monologues. He died in Beverly Hills at the age of sixty-five.

"Oscar, you're a great wit," Jack Paar began when Levant made one of his many appearances on Paar's talk show in 1958.

"Wits say two or three good things in their lives," Levant replied. "But humorists, like you, are the ones who are funny most of the time. You know what a humorist is, don't you, Jack?"

"What?"

"A humorist is someone like you. Someone with four writers who ad-libs a show. You're so full of charm. That's something I never stoop to."

Levant is modest in his accounting, as he said considerably more than two or three good things. "He'll double-cross that bridge when he comes to it," he quipped of a politician. Of a banker: "He's a self-made man. Who else would help?" On his first wife: "Neither one of us was too good for the other. Beside incompatibility, we hated each other." Furthermore, "marriage is a triumph of habit over hate." He famously defined chutzpah as "that quality which enables a man who has murdered his mother and father to throw himself on the mercy of the court as an orphan." Witticisms like that one made the jump into common sense, and of that he noted that "imitation is the sincerest form of plagiarism."

Oscar Levant's place in the pantheon of wit was assured by Dorothy Parker, who made his life the subject of her last piece of writing. In 1964, one year before his death and three before hers, she wrote an extended caption for two photographs of Levant in a book by Roddy McDowell.

"Over the years, Oscar Levant's image—that horrible word—was of a cocky young Jew who made a luxurious living by saying mean things about his best friends and occasionally playing the piano for a minute if he felt like it," she wrote. The real Levant had neither humility nor self-pity, she continued, and he wasn't in the least bit mean. So why did he come off that way? Groucho Marx had a theory.

"Levant was a little tough for me to take for I don't care for the gent in any form," Marx wrote to his daughter after seeing the film *Rhapsody in Blue*.

"You can have his comedy too as far as I am concerned. He has a brittle hardness and rudeness that just irritates me."

Levant blamed his subconscious for that ugly stuff, and even Freud ought to give him a pass on his terminology: For Levant, the unconscious was a pill-induced state. As he writes, quite disconcertingly in what was marketed as a comic memoir, "during the most acute phases of my mental depression, which lasted many years, my most unabated obsession was instant unconsciousness."

To Levant, the subconscious was the origin of wit, whether he liked it or not. More often than not, not.

"While we were sitting in the Brown Derby one day," Levant writes of a conversation with a composer. "I said 'Vernon, at your best'—and then my cynical subconscious reared its ugly head—'Cole Porter is better.' I hadn't meant it to come out in just that way."

It frequently came out worse, like when an errant jibe cost him his talk show. As he recounts it in *The Memoirs of an Amnesiac*: "The week that Arthur Miller and Marilyn Monroe were remarried by a rabbi I said—in my rambling, stream-of-consciousness manner—'Now that Marilyn Monroe is kosher, Arthur Miller can eat her.'"

He didn't mean it like *that*, he protested, but his show was immediately canceled. The furor became what Levant called "the most controversial case since Adolf Hitler presented his lovable nature to the public in 1923. There was a similarity."

Why did he say it? "I suspect my subconscious had led me to saying something outrageous enough to be thrown off the air," and back into a drugged haze.

A desire to shock, even to the point of self-sabotage, explains some of his witticisms. But it went deeper, as he himself noted after a particularly telling exchange with Noël Coward in 1954.

"How are you?" the British playwright inquired upon a chance meeting at a train station.

"Not too well," Oscar replied. "I'm slightly neurotic, you know."

"Oh, you Americans are all neurotic," Coward replied with a shrug.

"I answered with a remark which was inexplicable. I said, 'But I'm not an American.' [Levant's wife] June dragged me away in horror and disbelief."

If this was Oscar Levant's subconscious incoherently betraying him, we might assume the rest of his bon mots are the product of his subconscious pleasing its master. Levant's talent was not well-reasoned remarks that resulted from careful deliberation; he was fast off the mark. Unlike humor, wit is a speed game. If comedy is tragedy plus time, wit is comedy minus time. It's not surprising that his instantaneous quips would occasionally sound nonsensical, but it is proof that there was no calcula-

tion or planning involved. He made his way into the league of Great Wits with much less calculation than most, but there was nothing virtuous about this. His lines are Freud's involuntary inspiration personified. As Levant rightly told Paar, he was not a

humorist. He wasn't desperately trying to come up with new jokes; if anything, he tried to stop his mouth from running.

So Oscar Levant tells us that his wit emerged uncontrollably from his subconscious, meaning his unconscious. As armchair psychoanalysts—is there any other kind?—let's do a bit of black-box testing. What were the stimuli, the factors that went into creating Levant's unconscious? And what reactions, other than a lifetime of snappy one-liners that often snapped back, did it produce?

You Get Out What You Put In

First, the inputs. There was an unhappy childhood, one that made him say that when he grew up, he wanted to be an orphan. As the youngest of four sons in a devout family, his bar mitzvah—that momentous occasion on which a Jewish boy becomes a man—was held at eight a.m. on a Thursday with only his grandfather in attendance. No speech was made and he received no gifts. "It didn't bother me at the time," he notes dryly.

Music was of utmost importance in the Levant home and young Oscar's talents were encouraged, to a point. During one recital to friends and family, Oscar played his father's selections save for the encore, when he switched the Chopin for Beethoven. After he finished the piece and accepted his applause from the assembled, his father walked over and slapped him across the face.

This gave him a lifelong phobia of public performance, a distinct liability for a musician. Levant collected phobias like a pocket collects lint. There were the obvious ones, like death and the number 13, but also an array of uniquely irrational fears. Among them were:

- *Tchaikovsky's* 1812 Overture. As a young boy, Oscar's mother took him to an outdoor concert by the Pittsburgh Symphony. In the middle of this piece, a thunderstorm began, the audience ran for cover and Oscar nearly suffocated with the thought that he would lose his mother in the crowd. He not only cringed at the thought of this piece, but forever after refused to play his hometown.

- *Lemons.* Before Levant dropped out of high school at fifteen, he was "flat-footed, pigeon-toed, knock-kneed and lacked a certain grace," but he mustered the strength to enter a contest at a school dance. He was ecstatic as he waltzed toward victory—but mortified when the coach came out and gave him a lemon, the booby prize. "I don't allow a lemon on my table to this day," he wrote.

- *Roses.* His first sweetheart, a girl named Rose, died suddenly while Levant was off playing in New York. The result: "When someone sent roses (rose was the key word), I went into an absolute catatonic rigidity of despair."

- *Beet juice.* Spilling the red liquid on a tablecloth at his wealthy aunt's house created a lifelong aversion to the vegetable in all its forms.

- *Watches.* After his mother died, a wristwatch inscribed with Oscar's name was found among her effects. It was, presumably, a present for the bar mitzvah that wasn't.

Once he learned to fear, he just kept adding to this list. It was only when his professional life wound down that his phobias began to as well. The best therapy, it turned out, was writing them all down in his memoirs.

Then, the outputs. What else did Levant's subconscious produce? And what didn't it produce? Music is the answer to both those questions. Levant began his career as a pianist, honing his skills in both roadhouses and concert halls, the result being that he could instantly play just about any piece of music put in front of him. He could also improvise. "I had developed into what was called a flash pianist, full of technical ornamentation, appoggiaturas and cascading frills, but in the jazz lexicon, signifying absolutely nothing," he said with a Shakespearean flourish.

As Sam Kashner and Nancy Schoenberger write in their definitive biography, *A Talent for Genius: The Life and Times of Oscar Levant*, this talent was on full display in the 1927 Broadway play *Burlesque*: "When the play opened and Oscar began to feel comfortable in the role, he would often change songs, switching a new Gershwin or Jerome Kern number for one of the set pieces, sometimes interpolating refrains and melodies which he might have heard only that afternoon on a brief visit to T. B. Harms [music publishers]."

His ability to improvise was a great talent for a pianist, but it's even more important for a wit. Levant developed these skills concurrently, so it's possible that one fed into the other. To further explore that possibility, consider what vibrant wit and musical fluidity have in common: the ability to improvise. And as we learned from Halpern, Close and Johnson, to improvise you need to turn off the part of your mind that inhibits you from saying risky things, things you haven't completely thought out and that might result in the cancellation of your talk show.

To get physical, albeit simply, what Freud called the ego might correspond to the dorsolateral prefrontal cortex. That's the part of the brain that lights up when risks are being weighed. When a jazz musician is hooked up to a functional MRI and asked to improvise (as per the studies we discussed in "Flow") this area shows a marked decrease in activity—in other words, there's likely less of a filter on what your brain comes up with. Simultaneously next door in the medial prefrontal cortex, a part of the brain associated with individuality and self-expression, there's a fireworks show in progress.

It would be tempting, as budding Freudians and amateur neurologists, to call the one area of the brain the ego and the other the unconscious, but that's simplifying quite a bit. For one thing, psychology has come quite far since the Viennese witch doctor, and for another, neurobiology has quite far to go. Better just to focus on the links between Levant's verbal and musical freestyling, and to consider how a brain that's good at the one may also master the other.

That's not to say Levant couldn't write it down, though, at least musically. His skills at composition were honed under the great Arnold Schoenberg, and for a time in the mid-1930s, he looked down on all forms of music but serious orchestral pieces. It was during this time he composed "Blame It on My Youth," a jazz standard that became his most enduring work. He did so while eschewing jazz and movie soundtracks, claiming that he aspired to classical greatness. That he had the raw talent was universally acknowledged, and his overbearing parents did everything they could to give him the drive. And yet, perhaps fittingly, "Blame It on My Youth" is his sole major contribution to the American songbook.

So why weren't some major classical works part of his sub- and/or unconscious's output? One possibility is that energy he might have devoted to a magnum opus was frittered away in quips and insults. The suspicion that wit comes at the expense of greater creative endeavors is a popular one, exemplified today most clearly in Fran Lebowitz. After making her name in the late 1970s with two slim volumes of collected magazine columns, she's become more famous for all that she hasn't written than anything she has. And, of course, for her clever sayings, which have been likened to Levant's. When Lebowitz is asked about her lack of an oeuvre, she happily declares herself the laziest person in America. (When asked why she would consent to an interview about her sloth, she replied that "anything's better than writing.")

Though Levant had many problems, laziness wasn't one of them. More likely, the reason for his minimal output was George Gershwin. Levant was utterly infatuated with the famous composer, and when Gershwin died suddenly of an inoperable brain tumor at the age of thirty-eight, Levant devoted his career to being Gershwin's Best Friend, even playing that role in Warner Bros.' 1945 biopic *Rhapsody in Blue*. In that film, he remarks that "[i]f it wasn't for George, I could have been a pretty good mediocre composer." (As his obituary in *Time* put it, "except for Gershwin's music, Levant tended to pound the instrument like the back of an old crony.") Instead he was a great wit, and for all his neuroses and anxieties, he didn't regret that. For the most part, he didn't understand it, either.

What's Going On in There?

For all Oscar Levant's charm as a case study, the fact his brain didn't understand itself makes him hard to learn from. Ideally, we should hear from wits who knew how their intuition worked.

Keith Olbermann, the sportscaster turned newsman turned sportscaster, has built a career on his ability to instantly access a wealth of esoteric knowledge. Like Levant, he's such a famously difficult personality that this ability is the reason he has a career. Rather than wait for Olbermann to donate his brain to science, we can look to that brain's own insights on itself.

"I have a leafy brain, according to the theory of the leafy brain," he told *Esquire* in 2014. "I associate things that many people never put together."

It's unclear if there even is such a theory outside of Olbermann's leafy brain—in scientific parlance, it refers to a kind of fungus—but it's something he comes back to in interviews.

Way back in 1993, when describing his colleague Chris Berman to the Hartford *Courant*, he set it up like so:

"Now, there's an old theory which says that references and associations are the function of the number of tendrils there are in the neural centers of one's brain. The tendrils can look like a hand with five fingers sticking out, or they can look like a leaf with 105 sticking out."

This is most useful as a guide to how such a brain understands itself: Leafy. Though it's unclear how an overgrown mental forest produces the right line at the right time.

As a group, and as we'd expect, writers are quite good at describing how ideas bubble up from the inner recesses of the mind. Unfortunately, they are uniformly mystified as to the schedule on which this happens. In his interview with the *Paris Review*, Martin Amis recalls the days when passports had a spot to declare one's occupation, and so foreign correspondents would fill in the word "writer," knowing that if trouble arose they could round out the letter "r" to become waiters.

"I always thought there was great truth there. Writing is waiting, for me certainly," he says. "The job seems to be one of making yourself receptive to whatever's on the rise that day."

This, all the greats agree, is how literary inspiration works. In conversation, ideas that emerge on a daily basis are nowhere near quick enough: They lead to *l'esprit d'escalier*, having great comebacks that come forward too late to be of any use, a phenomenon we'll explore in our chapter on Resilience.

A better source is a mind trained to work in the moment, a mind like Steve Martin's. As a writer, actor, comedian and musician, he's adept in all the creative fields we've examined in this chapter. Here's how he describes his stand-up years in his memoir:

> *My most persistent memory of stand-up is of my mouth being in the present and my mind being in the future: the mouth speaking the line, the body delivering the gesture, while the mind looks back, observing, analyzing, judging, worrying, and then deciding when and what to say next.*

He drew from years and years of bits, the leaves of his brain, but knowing what to use when—or when it was time to ad-lib and grow a new leaf—was up to intuition. The beauty of how it works, again, is that you never quite know. If we were to solve the riddle of intuition, we'd effectively know ourselves too well. We'd be robots. At the end of his memoir, Martin expresses relief that his years of ad-libbing and spontaneity have yet to yield a perfect sense of what works. He explains how he determines if something is funny:

> *I picture myself in the back of a darkened theater, watching the bit in question unspooling on the screen, and somewhere, in the black interior of my brain, I can hear the audience's response. Thankfully, when the movie is finally screened, I discover that my intuition is not always right. If it were, there would be no surprises left; I would be living in a dull comedy heaven.*

So do we simply end by deciding to celebrate intuition because it's indeed worthy of celebration, or because we've realized we just can't figure it out? As an improviser would say: Yes.

{ QUIP QUIZ }

1. "It's best to work off the _____ when you have something up your sleeve."   **—George Murray**

2. "You beat your pate, and fancy wit will come: Knock as you please, there's nobody at _____."

    —Alexander Pope, "An Empty House"

3. "_____ consists in knowing how far to go in going
   too far."   **—Jean Cocteau**

4. "I used to think that the _____ was the most
   fascinating part of the body. Then I realized, look who's
   telling me that."   **—Emo Philips**

5. "Intuition is unconscious accumulated _____
   informing judgement in real time."   **—Alain de Botton**

Experience	Brain	Tact	Home	Cuff

INTUITION
WIT
LIST

☐ Freud says that some
   people just don't have
   a capacity for wit

☐ But you're not
   one of those people

☐ Say what's on your mind
   (as long as it won't
   ruin your life)

☐ Don't trim the branches
   of your leafy brain

FOUR

Confidence

Featuring: SWEDISH DRIVERS, INCOMPETENT CORNELL STUDENTS, OSCAR WILDE KICKING ASS, THE ATLANTIC OCEAN, OSCAR WILDE TAKING NAMES AND GOING TO JAIL

◆ ◆ ◆

Once you've done your Hustle—read your Wodehouse, watched your *Arrested Development* and otherwise completed enough of a cultural boot camp to prepare you for erudition—and figured out how to turn off the background noise in your central nervous system and just Flow, and determined just how much you can trust that little guy in your head we're calling Intuition, well, let's be honest: You're pretty much there. If you have the tools and the wherewithal to use them, wit is right in front of you. If it were a snake, it would bite you. So what follows is all about finessing: Applying the power of wit to the right times and places, seeing what it can and cannot do, and fiddling with the dials until the repartee is right where you want it to be.

What you've thus far done is constructed a self that's ready to see some cocktail-party action. Now you need to put that self out there. And how do you put yourself out there? With confidence.

If the research is to be believed, the vast majority of the public has no need for instruction in how to be confident.

The most famous proof of this came in a 1981 Swedish psychology paper evocatively titled "Are We All Less Risky and More Skillful Than Our Fellow Drivers?" The obvious answer to such a question is no: If words have any meaning, we can't all be better than everyone else. But in practice, and repeatedly in studies since, most of us say yes. This is such a trope that it's even been called out as such in a Dave Barry column. ("It's a well-known fact that all humans consider themselves to be above-average drivers, including primitive Amazonian mud people who have not yet discovered the wheel," he wrote in 2004.) It's called illusory superiority, or, if you prefer your folksy humor with a public-radio twang, the Lake Wobegon effect, the town from Garrison Keillor's *A Prairie Home Companion* where all the children are above average. This doesn't necessarily mean we all think we're great, just that we know that, whatever average might be, we're better than *that*.

A closely related concept—one that won its poor discoverers the IgNobel Prize—is called the Dunning-Kruger effect. It finds that incompetent people often judge themselves pretty good at things they know nothing about. Students were asked to rate various statements based on how funny they were—and their ability to perceive what's funny as compared to the average Cornell student. These were previously tested on professional comedians and rank from a 9.6 out of 11 for the very funny words of Jack Handey ("If a kid asks where rain comes from, I think a cute thing to tell him is 'God is crying.' And if he asks why God is crying, another cute thing to tell him is 'probably because of something you did.'") to a 1.3 out of 11 for a rather lame riddle of uncertain provenance (What is as big as a man but weighs nothing? His shadow.).

Those at the bottom of the barrel dramatically overestimated their ability to discern humor, even as they chose the duds and discarded the gems. Essentially, they figure that if they don't know much about the topic, why would anyone else? Amusingly, this same effect works in reverse on the other side of knowledge: Educated people often underestimate how much they know. If they know so much about the subject, surely everyone else does.

In a sense, the Lake Wobegon effect is actually the opposite of the Dunning-Kruger effect: In the first, everyone assumes they are above average. In the second, everyone roughly thinks they're average. In both, though, it's clearly a minority that has an accurate read on their ability.

And therein lie the two prongs of confidence: Are you good at a certain thing, and do you believe you're good at it? You might think it only matters that you are objectively good, but of course, that alone is not going to make you challenge yourself. Ideally, then, you might be quantifiably very good at something and then believe you are even slightly better, because who's to say you can't get better in the process of rising to the occasion? The drivers leaving the Swedish psychology lab may well have been more alert and conscientious on the way home than on the way in. But how do you know this? A good self-test is to ask yourself if you've been overly confident and then brought down a peg or two already. If so, you may well be on the route to genuine knowledge.

And now, via a brief plow through psychology, we come to Oscar Wilde: A man who was clearly very good at being witty, and was quite aware that he was good at it. But, as everyone familiar with even the broad strokes of his life knows, he was far too confident in his abilities. The fact that his biography had such a dramatic arc has certainly helped burnish his legend, and he saw it coming: Late in life in a letter he rechristened himself "St. Oscar of Oxford, Poet and Martyr." Before that, his brash confidence in his wit made him the brightest star of his age.

But Was He Any Good?

Many artists die in obscurity and achieve fame posthumously; the luckier ones become famous in their lifetimes and more so thereafter. Oscar Wilde managed to do all of the above. In his life, he symbolized the decadent movement in fin de siècle England; his homosexuality was a public secret that added to his infamy but didn't eclipse it (at least, not until it destroyed his career). After his death, he became a sort of folk hero: gay, Irish, well-spoken and the author of at least one undiminished masterpiece, *The Importance of Being Earnest*, and several essays that still sizzle off the page.

But it must be said: He wasn't always that good. A dive into his collected maxims shows an almost childish formula at play.

He hasn't a single redeeming vice, he said. Also: Give me the luxuries and anyone can have the necessities. And: I can believe anything, provided that it is quite incredible. As well: Familiarity breeds consent. Furthermore: He is old enough to know worse.

You could write a formula capable of coining these phrases, along the lines of:

Take common maxim, e.g., "X is the curse of the Ying classes," where X is drink and Y is work.

Substitute X for Y and vice versa.

Present new formulation with slight smile and twinkle in eye.

Or more regularly:

The definition of X is that it's Y, where Y is the opposite of X.

As in, punctuality is the thief of time.

Furthermore, it's arguable that he doesn't satisfy either half of our definition of wit as spontaneous creativity. His major works are certainly original, but elsewhere in his oeuvre you'll find blatant rip-offs of both his fellow poets and his own work. "To arrive at what one really believes, one must speak through lips different from one's own," he writes in "The Critic as Artist," an essay that itself borrows language from other critics. This has put Wilde scholars in a bind: Is his plagiarism a high-minded joke and a sort of meta-statement that nothing is truly original? Or was he a journeyman writer who had to churn out copy so quickly he had no choice but to borrow from whatever was at hand? Either way, the basic idea of creativity as creation isn't quite there. He is constantly, unabashedly recycling, reworking and refining his own words. This both is and isn't spontaneity. He reworked previously successful lines to new occasions, and to all the world they may have seemed like fresh thoughts. This, as we have seen with Churchill, is par for the course with all the Great Wits.

He churned out as much copy as an adoring public would consume, and at his peak his public was insatiable. The critic Louis Kronenberger aptly notes that the lines "that are more striking than substantial might be called halforisms."

Furthermore, as he'd hoped, he's been canonized since his death. One of the small tragedies to befall witty people is that they will forever be quoted by the witless. Or misquoted, as per the line "Quotation is a serviceable substitute for wit," which is often attributed to Wilde but is actually a paraphrase of W. Somerset Maugham.

And indeed, with ninety-two attributed quips, Wilde remains the most quoted person in the 2012 edition of *The Oxford Dictionary of Humorous Quotations*, followed distantly by George Bernard Shaw. This acclaim comes at a cost.

The fact is there are more wannabe Wildes than any of the other Great Wits. Sure, all politicians fancy themselves Churchills, but thankfully there are only so many politicians. In every metropolitan area hip enough to serve absinthe, you're guaranteed to find Wilde devotees. He personifies the charming and witty side of the gay stereotype, and so there are plenty of bright young things hoping (or perhaps just assuming) that, to paraphrase a Stephen Fry line about sodomy, witty banter is as much a part of homosexuality as owning a Volvo is of being middle class. Sadly, it's not.

Having Said That

So why, if we've decided that Oscar Wilde as he is known today is more often than not a cliché of wit, are we going to forgive him and hold him aloft as a model to be emulated? Because of this gem among the many in *The Importance of Being Earnest*:

> LADY BRACKNELL: (*Pulls out her watch.*) Come dear.
> (*Gwendolyn rises.*) We have already missed five, if not six,
> trains. To miss any more might expose us to comment
> on the platform.

The world today is as full of Lady Bracknells as it was in Wilde's time, if not more so. To be a Bracknell is to be entirely concerned with the perceived propriety of things and distinctly unbothered by the way things actually are. Comments on the platform are all she worries about, though she has long forgotten why they concern her so. On the stage, she is often and best played in drag.

Wilde, on the other hand, went out of his way to show he didn't care what busybodies thought. He knew that people might sputter and gasp, but he knew that alone couldn't hurt him. As he declared to a hungry pack of newspaper reporters on the occasion of his visit to America, "The ridicule which aesthetes have been subjected to is the only way of blind unhappy souls who cannot find the way to beauty."

Oscar Wilde was all about being true to one's self, mainly because he saw no other way to be. "All imitation in morals and in life is wrong," he wrote. And once you had that truth, you might as well be vocal about it.

The Confident Aesthete

Once Wilde had written his best works, he had a reputation to protect him—to a point—but how did he become the toast of London before he'd written a single lasting word? In other words, when he was just like the rest of us, how did he get away with acting like Oscar Wilde?

His early life suggests that he had a combination of extremely supportive parents, an excellent education, a cosmopolitan environment and a series of challenges regular enough to toughen him up for the next one. By the time he was sixteen and a student at Trinity College, Dublin, he was a towering six feet three inches and had begun to display his public love for dandyism in speech, mannerism and dress. These two facts are quite possibly related, as though he was on occasion mocked for his effete passions, it wasn't a good idea to do so to his face.

Wilde biographer Richard Ellmann notes one possibly apocryphal story from Trinity College in which a bully sneered after Wilde read a poem in class. "Wilde went up to him and asked by what right he did so. The man laughed again, and Wilde struck him in the face." The two had it out and, "to general astonishment [Wilde] proved to have a devastating punch and utterly worsted his opponent."

Similarly, in his early years at Oxford, a group of students who had heard one of his early notorious remarks—"I find it harder and harder every day to live up to my blue china"—decided to smash said china and give Oscar a beating in the process. Four of the undergraduates broke into his room while their friends watched, and the result (as described in a classmate's memoirs) sounds like a Liam Neeson action movie: "To the astonishment of the beholders, number one returned into their midst propelled by a hefty boot-thrust down the stairs; the next received a punch in the wind that doubled him up onto the top of his companion below; a third form was lifted bodily from the floor and hurled onto the heads of the spectators. Then came Wilde triumphant, carrying the biggest of the gang like a baby in his arms." In a flourish in keeping with Wilde's character, he invited the presumably agog crowd to join him in sampling his assailants' liquor cabinets. Naturally, they accepted.

Oscar Wilde: Ass Kicker is not how we usually picture the poet, but it goes a long way toward explaining why he didn't mind what others thought of him. Their words were just words, and aggressive action could be met with a hefty boot thrust.

In addition to his physical strength, Wilde was presumably buoyed by the continued, overarching faith his mother had in him. Even when he had no viable career prospects, no potential heiress to marry and no family money to fall back on, she seized upon his winning a poetry prize as "a certainty of success in the future" that would allow him to "trust your own intellect, and know what it can do."

The famous Wildeism that the only thing worse than being talked about is not being talked about aptly describes his entry to London society. As a recent university graduate, he had yet to produce any writing of merit, and yet through skillful social maneuvering he was soon attending the best parties in the city. He squired around a series of famous actresses, often promising to cast them in plays he had yet to write. Most notably, he was a great admirer and friend of Lillie Langtry, an attractive young woman who almost instantly became the toast of the town based on little more than her looks. Soon after her first appearance at a high-society party, her face appeared on postcards and she was romantically linked to the Prince of Wales. Her association with Wilde helped them both. She gave him further reason to be discussed by others, while he urged her toward a stage career, and thus something to be famous for beyond fame itself. (As Hiltons and Kardashians can attest, this remains good advice.)

All the attention Wilde managed to garner was its own reward in that it earned him a parody in Gilbert and Sullivan's comic operetta *Patience* as Bunthorne. In fact, the role of the "fleshly poet" was likely based on aesthetes who preceded Wilde in fame and publication, but he managed to become so identified with the parody that he was asked to come to the United States on a lecture tour to support the New York production of *Patience*. This was perhaps the supreme validation of Wilde's confidence: He was caricatured as an artist before he'd actually created much art, and that caricature had earned him a trip to the New World.

There, the hype about his verbal dexterity was such that a

boatload of reporters sailed out to meet his ship and pepper him with questions. He was suitably humbled by the long trip, but that didn't stop the wayward press. They expected a wispy man of letters but instead met a giant wrapped in a fur-trimmed green coat. What did he think of the voyage, they asked, and he told them, in uncharacteristically plain English, that it hadn't been very interesting. Unsatisfied with this answer, they canvassed other passengers until they cobbled together a report that had Oscar loftily announcing that he was "not exactly pleased with the Atlantic. It is not so majestic as I expected," which they could then run under a headline that screamed "Mr. Wilde Disappointed with the Atlantic." By the time he made it through quarantine and to customs, he was ready to play their game. He announced, "I have nothing to declare except my genius."

Again, one of the remarkable facts of Wilde's life is that though he achieved fame before he'd earned it, he didn't hesitate to earn it, and then earn some more. His two early plays, *Vera; or The Nihilists* and *The Duchess of Padua* were critical and commercial flops ("*Vera* bad," a gleeful *Punch* magazine said of the former; Wilde himself later admitted the latter was "unfit for publication").

He soon married and had two sons, resulting in *The Happy Prince* in 1888, a book of children's stories that benefited from channeling Wilde's conversational tone. In 1890's *The Picture of Dorian Gray*, Wilde seems to accept and own his verbal dexterity when he describes how in conversation Lord Henry "played with the idea and grew wilful; tossed it into the air and transformed it; let it escape and recaptured it; made it iridescent with fancy and winged it with paradox."

Perhaps more important to his work, he had accepted his sexuality. Around the same time, the less-than-happily married man began having affairs with men. Lord Alfred Douglas came into Oscar's life in 1891, and they fell in love almost immediately.

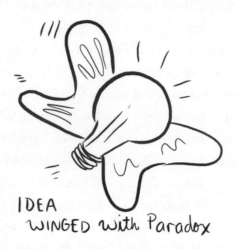

IDEA
WINGED with Paradox

The play *Lady Windermere's Fan* followed to much success, and then came *A Woman of No Importance*, *An Ideal Husband* and, finally, *The Importance of Being Earnest*. All were successes, and all went straight to Wilde's head. And also to his stomach: In the words of Kronenberger, "The gorging and the guzzling had helped make him, already an unattractive fat man, a very bloated and gross one: he not only went everywhere in hansoms [cabs], he found it a great struggle to get in and out of them."

Not to put too fine a point on it, but it's worth comparing the corresponding changes in his physical appearance and popular reception. As a vigorous young man, he took on bullies with his fists. As a bloated older man, he was much lazier about chastening those who taunted him. Indeed, it was at this time that a love letter to Douglas found its way to a blackmailer, the threats of whom Wilde discounted with a weak joke about his writing rarely commanding so high a price. The connection of flabby body and decaying mind is saved from being an irrelevant aside by the fact that the mind in question wrote *The Picture of Dorian Gray*, the definitive book on separating physical and mental atrophy.

Wilde's confidence at this stage was fully backed up by his work, but it continued to metastasize. Though homosexuality was illegal in Victorian England, it was unlikely to be prosecuted. But then a series of unlikely events occurred and Wilde responded to them in a manner so illogical it's likely both his overconfidence and love for Douglas were to blame.

In short order and without the cringing detail: Douglas's father, the Marquess of Queensberry, called Wilde a sodomite in a letter to his club. The wronged playwright, egged on by Alfred, sued Queensberry for libel. To get lawyers to take his case, he had to blatantly lie about his innocence. In court, he used his cross-examination as a stage for more aphorisms and halforisms, a highly inadvisable legal strategy. A procession of rent boys was brought out of the shadows, which flustered Oscar. When asked if he had kissed one of them, his immediate response was, "Oh, dear no. He was a peculiarly plain boy. He was, unfortunately, extremely ugly. I pitied him for it." At this point, one can imagine Wilde's lawyers smacking their foreheads. The best wit the Great Wit could summon was useless at this point. Why did he mention how ugly the boy was, the blood-smelling examiner inquired.

"If I were asked why I did not kiss a door-mat, I should say I do not like to kiss door-mats," Wilde sputtered, making things worse. "You sting me and insult me and try to unnerve me; and at times one says things flippantly when one ought to speak more seriously. I admit it."

This startling admission is basically his repentance for an artistic lifetime of silly statements, but that was obviously beside the point. After his unsuccessful libel trial and his trial for gross indecency, Wilde was sentenced to two years of hard labor. His physical health going into jail was compromised, and the rough life behind bars broke him down. "Three permanent punishments authorized by law: 1. Hunger, 2. Insomnia and 3. Disease" constitutes one of his prison observations you'll rarely encounter in a book of quotations. There was indeed something worse than not being talked about—being held in complete contempt.

In *Oscar's Books: A Journey around the Library of Oscar Wilde*, Thomas Wright offers a heartbreaking glimpse of just how savagely the public tore Oscar's life to shreds.

In April 1895, while Wilde was in prison between his trials, his creditors had all his personal effects auctioned off to pay the Marquess of Queensberry's legal fees. Among many literary prizes, the catalogue highlights "Old blue and white china" of the sort Wilde had once protected from bullies. Now, he was defenseless.

"At the auction, Wilde's 'House Beautiful' was plundered by a frenzied crowd of curiosity hunters who had come in search of mementoes of the 'monster,'" Wright writes. "During the sale, the white front door of No. 16 was left open, giving the jostling crowds access to the house and licence to loot it."

His valuable and rare books were indiscriminately bundled and sold for meager amounts, and many of his personal papers were trampled, stolen or illegally sold to a public eager for more descriptions of Wilde's decadent life.

It's difficult to end the story of Oscar Wilde on this note, even if that is roughly where his biological life concludes. He writes *De Profundis* and *The Ballad of Reading Gaol* from his time in prison, both of which are a lifetime away from his drawing-room plays. He then spends the rest of his days in France, where he has more affairs, drinks too much and, in the elegant words of Richard Ellmann, behaves "like a man waiting for something, perhaps a miracle, only to find that it is death." It came on November 30, 1900.

The Artifice of Being Interesting

For our purposes, the most interesting years of Wilde's life came after his graduation from Oxford but before he earned his literary fame. It was then that he made his name in London society, a name with little to back it up but his confidence that he certainly belonged there. To use Aristotle's logic, you become confident by acting confidently. Or as a twelve-step program would phrase it, fake it till you make it. This isn't to say Wilde was faking his wit—he had worked hard to ensure that he had a lifetime's worth of quips rehearsed and at the ready. He was well read and had been constantly reminded of his talent throughout his childhood. He had some success at school, though by no means in all fields. He knew his limitations and worked around them. But

> *He faked it till he made it, but then opted to continue faking it.*

he was assured that even as a newly graduated young Irishman with no great fortune or achievements to his name, he would be at home in the most elegant drawing rooms of the English-speaking world's cultural capital.

It's been said that Oscar Wilde lived his life in a sort of dream world, one that even the horrors of Victorian prison couldn't shatter. Jorge Luis Borges wrote that Wilde was "a man who keeps an invulnerable innocence in spite of the habits of evil and misfortune." That was in reference to his work, but it applies just as well to his life. Moments of self-doubt are all but absent from his biography. Even when he was writing bad poetry and racking up debts, he charged onward. Fame and fortune didn't change him so much as they caught up to the lifestyle to which he had long been accustomed.

To return to the famous measure of overconfidence, Oscar Wilde would surely be a better-than-average driver, even if the automobile wasn't invented until he was in his thirties. And on the Dunning-Kruger test, he would be sure to judge himself above average. But it's important to note that he never seemed to even bother with self-assessment, so sure was he of his rightful place in the world.

He was confident enough to know he would be somebody before he was somebody; confident enough to accept his literary fame as his due; and finally, confident enough to assume charm, wit and reputation would save him. He faked it till he made it, but then opted to continue faking it, as one might expect of a man who embraced artifice.

JACK: How you can sit there, calmly eating muffins when we are in this horrible trouble, I can't make out. You seem to me to be perfectly heartless.

ALGERNON: Well, I can't eat muffins in an agitated manner. The butter would probably get on my cuffs. One should always eat muffins quite calmly. It is the only way to eat them.

{ QUIP QUIZ }

1. "Success didn't spoil me; I've always been _____."

   —Fran Lebowitz

2. "The men who really believe in themselves can be found in _____."   —G. K. Chesterton

3. "Inspiration may be a form of super-consciousness, or perhaps of subconsciousness—I wouldn't know. But I am sure it is the antithesis of _____."

   —Aaron Copland

4. "Confidence is a _____ they can't wipe off."

   —Lil Wayne

5. "No one really feels self-confident deep down because it's an _____ idea."   —Russell Brand

| Insufferable | Lunatic asylums | Self-consciousness | Stain | Artificial |

CONFIDENCE
wit list

- ☐ Assume you're a Bad driver
- ☐ Overpromise. Overdeliver
- ☐ Ask someone critical to list all your flaws
- ☐ Ignore 90% of them
- ☐ Fake it
- ☐ Make it
- ☐ Don't go to jail

FIVE

Refreshment

Featuring: THE *ENOLA GAY*, A RANKING OF VARIOUS ALCOHOLS,

EWAN MCGREGOR'S BEST LINE, TALKING VS. WRITING AND

A DEFENSE OF A LIFE WITHOUT A MASTERPIECE

◆ ◆ ◆

Does drinking make you wittier? One might as well ask if witting makes you drinkier, which it may. Wit requires a diminishment of inhibition, perhaps the most prized of all alcohol's characteristics. Once any lingering social anxiety is washed away by a stiff drink, the brain–mouth connection is unimpeded. Instant confidence! Provided the brain knows what it's doing, the fireworks can begin.

That's a big proviso, one that explains why the Algonquin Round Table isn't re-created at every neighborhood tavern around the world on a nightly basis, and why it took TV's best writers' room to make *Cheers* work for eleven seasons. In addition, the quantity of alcohol required to liberate repartee is both minimal and exact, while the amounts needed to induce boorishness are

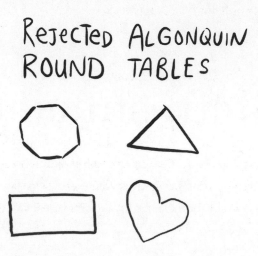

REJECTED ALGONQUIN ROUND TABLES

so various that even an amateur drinker will have no trouble finding them.

A quick glance over Mankind's Ten Stages of Drunkenness (as refined in Dan Jenkins's 1983 novel *Baja Oklahoma* and widely circulated elsewhere) explains this:

1. Witty and charming

2. Rich and powerful

3. Benevolent

4. Clairvoyant

5. F*** dinner

6. Patriotic

7. Crank up the *Enola Gay*

8. Witty and charming, part two

9. Invisible

10. Bulletproof ("The last stage was almost certain to end in a marriage.")

Though undeniably American—hence the World War II reference at stage seven—the dire progression of this list is sadly and universally true. In the book *Intoxication and Society*, British historian Philip Withington proves this with his vivid descriptions of drinking practices of the 1600s, a time when learned men were

expected to consume vast quantities of alcohol while retaining (if not sharpening) their critical faculties. He recounts one particularly resonant story of two lawyers and a cleric in Yorkshire who began their time in the alehouse with a faux-Latin competition (stage one) and ended it with one of the lawyers using his pipe to burn the cleric's exposed genitalia (stage ten, at least).

To the impartial and completely sober observer, only the first stage is objectively, verifiably true. The self-delusion sets in as early as stage two: You're poorer by the cost of at least two drinks, and it's only now that you feel rich? Progressive phases become harder for the outsider to distinguish as they tend to slur together, though stage three generally manifests itself in a few free drinks for the drunk's entourage. It's particularly important to note that stage eight, the second coming of wit, exists entirely in the mind of the subject and is most likely to start a bar fight. At no point will it result in aphorisms worth recording for posterity.

I'll Have What He's Having

So if a maximally witty state is induced by the first or second drink, depending on your body and brain mass, the all-important question then becomes, what should you drink? A low-alcohol beverage is perhaps the obvious answer, but the ratio of alcohol to water could lead the drinker to come up with the best zingers while in the ladies' room.

Barring rigorous scientific testing, our best guide is once again history. Herewith, a sliding scale from least appropriate beverage to most, with citations from the consumption patterns of the Great Wits.

Nothing at All

> *I don't drink liquor. I don't like it. It makes me feel good.*
> —Oscar Levant, closing the case on teetotaling

Beer

The famed British prints *Beer Street* and *Gin Lane* depict the former as a wholesome, patriotic beverage and the latter as a poison that leads to depraved acts. Aside from some vaguely good-natured merriment on Beer Street, it's not clear that either eighteenth-century characterization included wit. Look to the beer commercials of today and little has changed. Sophistication is rarely on display unless it's wearing a string bikini. The exception that proves the rule is "The Most Interesting Man in the World" campaign, designed in 2006 by the Euro RSCG Worldwide marketing firm for Dos Equis beer. The advertisements are a series of descriptors of a suave older gentleman, many of which work as stand-alone quips—"He once had an awkward moment, just to see how it feels," for instance. The tagline—"I don't always drink beer, but when I do, I prefer Dos Equis"—makes it clear that the only reason this works is that this guy is nothing like your average beer drinker.

Vodka

Tasteless, odorless, colorless—these are not the attributes of a wit. They more likely describe a spirit made with the express purpose of getting people sloshed, whether they be Russian peasants drinking it straight or sorority girls mixing it with Red Bull. Comrades, ladies: Can we call you a cab?

White Wine

Christopher Hitchens held this beverage in more contempt than any other, noting on one occasion that it didn't count as drinking and on another that he couldn't bear to hear it being ordered at a bar (though to be fair, he was talking about bad house wine). Also of note, the wittiest line in Roman Polanski's film *The Ghost Writer*, uttered by Ewan McGregor's character when, after an unbearable aperitif, he is finally offered Scotch: "White wine. Never saw the point of it."

Give the last word on white wine to Falstaff, one of literature's most famous drunks. In *Henry IV, Part II*, the rotund knight is being admonished for constantly sucking on his flask of sack, or "sec," dry white wine. He explains his necessary intoxication to Prince John:

> *A good sherry sack hath a two-fold operation in it. It ascends me into the brain, dries me there all the foolish and dull and crudy vapors which environ it, makes it apprehensive, quick, forgetive, full of nimble, fiery, and delectable shapes, which, delivered o'er to the voice, the tongue, which is the birth, becomes excellent wit.*

Red Wine

Slightly more committal than white. Stains your teeth, which may inhibit banter, though Dorothy Parker called it the Red Badge of Courage. More damningly, it is prone to induce conversations about varietals, robe, legs, terroir and other dull subjects best suited to the aisles of nicer liquor stores, the sort that employ people specifically to discuss these matters. As Fran Lebowitz observed, great people talk about ideas, average people talk about things and small people talk about wine. Once you remove the cork from the bottle, you may release all manner of inane banter.

Champagne

Sparkling, fizzy, effervescent—just as the descriptors of vodka denote a conversation best avoided, those of Champagne describe the best repartee. Regular wine is flat while Champagne (or prosecco, or straight sparking wine) is bubbly, like good conversation. Here, the expert to consult is Mark Twain, who, in an entirely straightforward letter to a scholar researching the drinking habits of great writers, noted the following: "I find that about two glasses of Champagne are an admirable stimulant to the tongue, and is, perhaps, the happiest inspiration for an after-dinner speech which can be found; but, as far as my experience goes, wine is a clog to the pen, not an inspiration."

Scotch

Winston Churchill's drink of choice, though he didn't drink much of it ("the daddy cocktail," as his daughter termed it, was the slightest drop of whiskey in a glass of water). The definitive ranking of all brown beverages is perhaps best replicated by the order W. C. Fields hit the drink over the course of his lifetime. He began with ginger ale and brandy, moved on to Scotch whisky, then to Irish whiskey, then bourbon and finally he went clear (though not in the Scientology sense) to martinis. Which brings us to . . .

Gin

The historical judgment in favor of this spirit is overwhelming for the simple reason that gin, in its most common English incarnation, was the beverage of choice for the great British wits of the seventeenth century. It helps that it's always been vaguely disreputable—once you're drinking it, you might as well say whatever you like. As Kingsley Amis wrote in *How's Your Glass?*: "[G]in had for many years a thoroughly unrespectable 'image,' not quite lost even today. Like Scotch whisky, and unlike vodka and white rum, gin is associated with people who like drink."

That said, a notable dissenter from the juniper-infused spirit was Dorothy Parker, who would order anything but. But still: The Martini!

The classic beverage of cocktail-party repartee has an exalted place on the bar of the wit, and for the most part it is deserved. First of all, if you're only having one or two drinks in an evening, they may as well count. As well, both martinis and wit are described as being at their best when served dry (though to be fair, this could have been said about white wine, but it wasn't, so we move on). And back to Hitchens, who memorably stated that one should "observe the same rule about gin martinis—and all gin drinks—that you would in judging female breasts: one is far too few, and three is one too many." Gin wins.

The Hitchens Exception

Many people drink more than Christopher Hitchens drank, and a few might be sharper tongued, but his particular combination of thirst and wit is shared by a very small crowd of people who likely shouldn't be invited to weddings, funerals or other ceremonies that call for long periods of solemnity. Hitchens loved the drink and wasn't shy about declaring it. Doesn't that imply he was an alcoholic? That concern was exactly the sort of thing he didn't have, and alcohol must be given due credit.

It is a brave man or woman who conducts a public life in the modern age while loudly celebrating alcohol. The more effusively one enjoys booze, the more society expects one drinks of it. But eloquence isn't measured by the shot glass, and those who drink the most generally do the least, both in slurred words and stumbly actions, to encourage the rest of us.

Hitchens labored not unhappily under the general suspicion he was a drunkard, likely realizing it at least meant he'd be forever greeted by well-stocked bars. In his memoir *Hitch-22*, he describes the "anxious, considerate way that my hosts greet me, sometimes even at the airport, with a large bottle of Johnnie Walker Black Label. It's almost as if they feel that they must propitiate the demon that I bring along with me. Interviewers arriving at my apartment frequently do the same, as if appeasing the insatiable."

In Ian Parker's memorable 2006 *New Yorker* profile, he concluded that his subject drank "like a Hemingway character: continually and to no apparent effect."

Hitchens credited booze with the very thing Twain claimed it could not give: He wrote that it "can help provide what the Greeks called *entheos*, or the slight buzz of inspiration when reading or writing." But there are shelves full of writers who make clear that alcohol is no help, and many more libraries devoid of books stolen by the bottle.

The late writer David Rakoff, working menial publishing jobs in New York at twenty-three, described the way his friends aspired to wit by drinking instead of writing. On *This American Life*, he explained their misery:

> *With enough $4 drinks sloshing through our veins, even the most dunderheaded schoolyard japery qualified as coruscating repartee. . . .*
>
> *Paying the bill we stumbled out into the street and back to our apartments, where we spent the rest of the night jealously reading the manuscripts of those who actually wrote and didn't just drink about it.*

Getting drunk in front of the typewriter just creates a whole new set of problems. John Irving made the point well to the *Paris Review* in 1986:

> *I'm not so down on drinking for writers from a moral point of view; but booze is clearly not good for writing or for driving cars. You know what Lawrence said: "The novel is the highest example of subtle interrelatedness that man has discovered." I agree! And just consider for one second what drinking does to "subtle interrelatedness." Forget the "subtle"; "interrelatedness" is what makes novels work—without it you have no narrative momentum; you have incoherent rambling. Drunks ramble; so do books by drunks.*

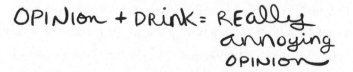

OPINION + DRINK = REALLY annoying OPINION

Talking vs. Writing

Why was Hitchens different? Because he worked constantly. Because while he was rarely subtle, he was never incoherent. And because as a writer, he was really a talker. Alcohol may not improve writing, but moderate amounts of it certainly improve conversation. If writing is just a way of talking to people via a printed page, then it follows that whatever improves your speech should do the same for your prose.

Most writers aren't talkers, though, and for good reason. They've chosen a means of expression that allows them time to look up references, revise their work and clearly think out what it is they want to say. Their dialogue takes place on both the silent page and their own terms. Alcohol would only slow this process, if not derail it entirely.

Hitchens, by contrast, had the sort of mind that already knew what it wanted to say. He was amazingly well read, but, more to the point, the things he had read were well thought-out. This explains his voluminous output, though the ability to offer up obscure references, quotations and mots justes on the page can never be as impressive as the impromptu ability to do so. He could write fast but talk faster. Hitchens recounts early guidance from the journalist Simon Hoggart, who "informed me that an article of mine was well argued but dull, and advised me briskly to write 'more like the way that you talk.'" The caveat is that this advice is only useful to those who really know how to talk. There was never any doubt that Hitchens was among their number.

As his close friend Martin Amis put it: "He thinks like a child (that is to say, his judgments are far more instinctive and moral-visceral than they seem, and are animated by a child's eager apprehension of what feels just and true); he writes like a distinguished author; and he speaks like a genius."

Of his thinking, this reliance on intuition and animating passion are among the primary virtues of alcohol. A moderate dose of booze—and it's hard to overstate how important the word "moderate" is here—clears your head of the convoluted and the confusing, washing away free-floating anxiety and bringing the things you actually care about into raised relief. This is almost a playbook for the Hitchens argument.

Of his good writing and better talking, pen and paper only slowed him down; if you could get him over to your house, you could put his books down.

Which explains why Hitch was quite in his element on television, a fact he owns up to with some dismay in *Hitch-22*.

> *[E]very time I go into a TV studio, I feel faintly guilty. This is pre-eminently the "soft" world of dream and illusion and "perception": it has only a surrogate relationship to the "hard" world of printed words and written-down concepts to which I've tried to dedicate my life, and that surrogate relationship, while it, too, may be "verbal," consists of being glib rather than fluent, fast rather than quick, sharp rather than pointed. It means reveling in the fact that I have a meretricious, want-it-both-ways side. My only excuse is to say that at least I do not pretend that this is not so.*

(Or as London Mayor Boris Johnson phrased the same idea in a different context: "My policy on cake is still pro–having it and pro–eating it!")

A Masterpiece at the Bottom of His Glass

This goes to the heart of Hitch, and it's the sort of balance that very few artists can manage. Either you're out in the world, drinking life to its lees, or you're sequestered in your garret, typing furiously from the confines of your mind. He's certainly right that the best way to have it is both ways, neat and on ice, with an olive and with a twist of lemon, sometimes writing, usually talking, always drinking.

On balance, though he wanted it both ways, he spent the most successful portion of his career living and working in the moment. Decades of being a professional gadfly paid off with *God Is Not Great*, his 2008 anti-theist tract. Before then, he'd taken book-length shots at the likes of Bill Clinton, Henry Kissinger and Mother Teresa—unfortunately, it must here be noted that the title of that last one was *The Missionary Position*—but in hindsight those seem like mere warm-ups. He also had to surprise and aggravate his lifelong fellow travelers by supporting the Iraq War, a stance that was as principled as it was career-boosting. That's when the televised Hitch truly entered the popular imagination. In an ascendant cable-news ecosystem filled with smiling chatterboxes and tinpot pundits, a deeply eloquent Oxford-caliber debater was the apex predator. He could always talk but now he was saying something that everyone wanted to hear, even if they found it abhorrent.

The success of *God Is Not Great* would seem to favor the writing Hitch, but in fact it was his talking platform that launched and sustained it. Religious groups around the United States, secure in their devotion, invited him to debate priests,

> *The best way to have it is both ways, neat and on ice, with an olive and a twist of lemon.*

pastors, church elders and rabbis. He walked into the houses of God, insulted the landlord, sold piles of books to the tenants and generally left everyone happy with the transaction. The book was the libretto, worth owning to remind you of the opera.

This is characteristic of the Greats and helps to secure Hitchens's place among them. "Those who'd heard Wilde talk found reading his written words disappointing; rather like drinking yesterday's wine," writes Ralph Keyes in his collection of the Irishman's epigrams. "The words were there, but the spirit was missing: the lilt, the sparkle, the daring leaps from one topic to the next. Some of Wilde's best lines occurred only during conversation." This was indeed an almost universally held opinion. By comparison, Christopher Hitchens was lucky to live into the age of YouTube.

He died of esophageal cancer in 2011, a disease certainly aided by years of smoking and likely abetted by all that drinking. There's no case to be made that aspiring wits follow his model of substance abuse, but it's equally futile to argue that he should have tempered his addictions. The bon vivant is by definition on the side of life's quality over quantity. If an unpleasant alcoholic favors drink over people, Hitchens loved drink as a way to engage with his fellow man.

In *Hitch-22*, the person dearest to Christopher Hitchens is clearly his mother, Yvonne. In his description of her, he unwittingly—no, actually and characteristically, completely wittingly—synthesizes a life of passion, conviction and pleasant inebriation. It's only fair to give him the last words:

"She was the cream in the coffee, the gin in the Campari, the offer of wine or champagne instead of beer, the laugh in the face of bores and purse-mouths and skinflints, the insurance against bigots and prudes."

{ QUIP QUIZ }

1. "Do not allow your children to mix drinks. It is unseemly and they use too much _____." —Fran Lebowitz

2. "Drinking whiskey is a form of amputation; four fingers, three fingers, two fingers. Luckily I have two _____." —George Murray

3. "Some weasel took the _____ out of my lunch." —W. C. Fields

4. "An _____ is someone you don't like who drinks as much as you do." —Dylan Thomas

5. "Drugs and alcohol are not my problem—_____ is
   my problem."
   —Russell Brand

Vermouth	Hands	Cork	Alcoholic	Reality

The WIT LIST

☐ Drink two glasses of champagne or a solid martini

☐ Be Christopher Hitchens

☐ Forget producing a masterpiece. Focus on getting off a really good line about the latest must-watch TV show

☐ Have a designated driver

SIX

Righteousness

Featuring: SAMUEL L. JACKSON IN *PULP FICTION*,
LOUIS C.K., THE BUS TO PITTSBURGH,
SYDNEY SMITH AND GEORGE BERNARD SHAW

◆ ◆ ◆

The difference between being right and being righteous is the difference between knowing the score and broadcasting it. There is, in theory and among the fully self-actualized, some smug satisfaction to be gained from being bathed in the light of the truth while the rest of humanity wanders around in darkness, tripping over falsehoods, stubbing their toes on conventional wisdom and swearing at typos. But that satisfaction only lasts so long, and then the hands of the wise reach for the megaphone. They just want to help the masses, they reason, though of course letting those masses know how enlightened their helpers are must be part of the appeal.

So if you're going to be right and righteous, you need to be ready to talk when that megaphone is positioned before your lips. How can you convey your message so it resonates? What can you say to let the people know your truth is the one that really deserves that capital T?

If all this talk of sharing the truth (and capitalizing it) sounds a touch religious, well, it should. The word "righteousness" and its variants are used in many of the world's religions and, for that matter, its atheist movements. It combines being right with being just, moral, true, upright, sincere and heaven-bound. "The path of the righteous man is beset on all sides by the inequities of the selfish and the tyranny of evil men," Jules Winnfield tells his victims in *Pulp Fiction*, crediting this thought to Ezekiel 25:17 when in fact it's the work of director Quentin Tarantino—no such verse appears in the Bible. (Rewatching the movie with this knowledge only makes it better.) The Righteous Brothers are the best reason to watch *Top Gun*.

Organized religion can draw upon the carrot of eternal salvation and the stick of eternal damnation to get its message across. Throw in tribal loyalties and meaningful tradition and you've pretty much earned your tax-exempt status. But what if you don't have or don't want to use those sweeteners? What if your message is based purely on cold hard logic? Or if you're sure people should hear your truths for no reason beyond the simple fact that they're true?

Then you dress it up a bit, make it entertaining for the listeners, and channel that righteousness into wit.

The Righteous Degenerate

As a rule of thumb, those deeply concerned with the state of the human soul usually don't make fart jokes. Or at least, not funny ones. But for one man, there is a strong connection between the two. The fart-soul tension is what underpins all Louis C.K.'s work.

First, farts. As he told *Time* magazine, he is not only not above a joke about flatulence, but he's frankly offended by anyone who would be. As he reasoned, "farts come out of your ass and they make a fucking trumpet sound. That shit-smelling gas comes out of your ass and it makes a toot sound. What the fuck is not funny about that? It's perfect, it's a perfect joke. It has all the elements."

This is true, at least by stand-up comedian logic, if not that of the person sitting next to you on a packed transatlantic flight. But it also plays to the first of two seemingly contradictory, but in fact complementary, sides of Louis: Namely, that he is a crass, lazy slob.

Some examples from his many stand-up appearances and interviews:

- "The meal is not over when I'm full. The meal is over when I hate myself." (*Chewed Up*, 2008)

- "I ate too much and masturbated recently, you know? It's bad to, like, jerk off and run out the door, 'cause you run into somebody. 'Oh, she knows. . . .' You've got to take some time alone to process the shame." (*Chewed Up*, 2008)

◆ "I've started to kind of hate people, and it's not because I have anything against them. It's just, I enjoy it. It's recreation." (*Shameless*, 2007)

OK, so it seems like we've come a long way from dinner-party bon mots. But then we get to the other half of the act, the other side of C.K., the part where he reminds us that we are tremendously, improbably, stupidly lucky to be alive. For instance:

◆ "Out of all the people that ever were, almost all of them are dead. There are way more dead people, and you're all gonna die and then you're gonna be dead for way longer than you're alive. Like that's mostly what you're ever gonna be. You're just dead people that didn't die yet." (*Hilarious*, 2011)

◆ "I have a feeling dead people get really mad when we complain about losing hair." (Reddit, 2012)

◆ "It seems like the better it gets, the more miserable people become. There's never been a technological advancement where people think, 'Wow, we can finally do this!'" (*Vanity Fair*, 2009)

All of these bits are great in isolation; indeed, they're enough to make him one of the finest comedians working today. But it's how they combine that really makes him a righteous force. No one wants to be told they aren't worthy of their comfortable way of life. There's a moral overtone to that, hence the expression "holier than thou." At the same time, everyone is happy to nit-pick their fellow man. The reason every religion has its own version of the Golden Rule is that it's very easy to ignore. Just telling people they ought to treat others as they'd like to be treated doesn't work terribly well, so if you want to impart that righteous message, you need a better strategy.

Louis C.K.'s is this: He not only opens himself up for scrutiny but scrutinizes himself in much harsher terms than anyone else could. Emphasizing his most pathetic moments knowingly blurs the line between soliciting laughs of recognition and laughs of horror. So then, when he segues into generalized complaints about us, as in modern humanity, well, you know he's not lecturing. Or he is, but from our level or perhaps a bit below us, and that makes all the difference.

"Everything Is Amazing and Nobody Is Happy."

That's the core of Louis C.K.'s famous rant about our technology and ourselves, delivered in his stand-up special *Hilarious* and in slightly different forms in talk-show appearances. It is perhaps the defining Louis bit: The smirking spokesman of "the worst generation so far," railing against entitlement and our extinct sense of wonder. This is a good sort of righteousness, delivered by a guy who freely admits he only stops eating when he hates himself. In other words, he's not saying he's better than us but rather that we could all stand to be a bit better.

His act is comedy but he freely admits he's not only up there to make people laugh. Or rather, laughing is just one way to get the reaction he's interested in, one of "heightened response." As he told *Time*, he'll happily accept scaring people. He's aptly and offhandedly described our finite lives as like being on a bus to Pittsburgh, only you can never mention the destination for fear of being shushed by all the other passengers. "'God, you know, you're so obsessed with Pittsburgh,'" he says, imitating the shocked fellow passengers. "Well, it says it on the fucking tickets and on the front of the bus."

Any comedian who described himself as a truth teller would get the wrong kind of laughs, or more likely none at all. But there's a righteous anger at falsehoods at the core of Louis C.K.'s act. It's this insistence that we open our eyes that sets him apart from other comedians. You get the sense discomfort is his favorite way to get laughs. You also begin to understand why he hasn't succeeded by traditional paths: He directed the feature film *Pootie Tang* but had it radically re-edited by the studio, and the first incarnation of his television show (HBO's *Lucky Louie*) lasted a season before being canceled. His success is well deserved but, as even he admits, improbable.

"I'm a vulgar, fucked-up degenerate comedian who did drugs. And I'm connecting with Christian mothers and fathers," he marvels in 2006's *Dead-Frog* interview. "I love that. That means so much to me."

We are alive in the world and that matters: That's the common ground Christian mothers and fathers share with Louis. Oh, and those souls are attached to bodies that occasionally and noisily release foul gases. The flesh-and-blood form we take for the brief time we have on this planet comes equipped with this feature that, across all eras and cultures, is pretty funny. That's vulgar and it's righteous, and that combination is a horrible one for a prime-time sitcom or a big-budget movie. For a middle-aged bald guy, though, it works just fine.

The Holiest Wit

If you have truth to share, it helps if people listen. To get people to listen, it helps to leaven that truth with wit. Admittedly this is not the course chosen by many religious types. Though some have tried to tease humor out of the Bible, a rigorous review of their findings reveals that there isn't any. Irony, sure. Sarcasm, yeah. But laughs, no. The Old Testament is famously harsh, but even in the new book, Jesus didn't chuckle, snicker or guffaw; he wept.

Still, one of history's most famous wits was a clergyman. Admittedly he rarely made a joke of his work, and furthermore he only became a man of the cloth because he couldn't afford to go to medical school. Sydney Smith lived from 1771 to 1845, though his witticisms were commonly quoted well into the twentieth century. Indeed, he was the Churchill or Wilde of his day: His lines popped up in memoirs, biographies and popular histories in such quantity that they clearly couldn't have all been his. To modern ears they sound a bit creaky, but remember that wit rarely ages well, and what seems obvious now wasn't always thus.

When a doctor advised Smith to go for a walk on an empty stomach, he replied, "Whose?"

To a woman complaining of the heat: "It was so dreadful here that I found there was nothing left for it but to take off my flesh and sit in my bones."

And perhaps most tellingly, to his more somber and successful brother: "You and I are exceptions to the laws of nature. You have risen by your gravity, and I have sunk by my levity."

As a careerist, Smith is a horrible model. He was big on neither fire and brimstone nor chapter and verse. The religion he preached was about doing good and being happy. He never made it far up the ladder in the Church of England—the title of bishop was forever out of his grasp—but this was mainly so for the most admirable of reasons. He fought, loudly and publicly, for what he knew to be right. In his pamphlets, he attacked the high salaries of his fellow clergymen and argued that Catholics deserved full rights under the law. Of a particularly devout strain of Anglicans, he wrote that they practiced "a religion of postures and ceremonies, of circumflexions and genuflections, of garments and vestures, of ostentation and parade; that they took up the tithe of mint and cumin, and neglected the weightier matters of the law—justice, mercy and the duties of life."

It's no surprise that this hurt his advancement, but the key lesson of his life is that it only made him more popular in social circles because he made his points with wit. Reading his letters or having his company was entertaining, no matter his topic, and his light touch allowed him to broach the heaviest of subjects. You might not choose a radical as your dinner guest, but if he makes you laugh, who cares about his politics?

As he wrote to a friend:

What is real piety? What is true attachment to the Church? How are these fine feelings best evinced? The answer is plain: by sending straw-berries to a clergyman. Many thanks.

The Bearded Behemoth

If you want to set a difficult life goal for yourself, try this: Turn your last name into an adjective before you're fifty. Bonus points if you have a name that doesn't lend itself to being adapted this way and you're not a head of state ("Clintonian" is too obvious on both counts). By the time George Bernard Shaw was in his mid-forties, around 1900, it was possible to describe both his work and his imitators as Shavian.

As he explained in a preface to his play *Man and Superman*, he did this by "being a force of Nature instead of a feverish selfish little clod of grievances complaining that the world will not devote itself to making you happy."

In the first third of his life, George Bernard Shaw was both a committed atheist and a street preacher. His religion was social-ism, and as a founder of the Fabian Society—a group committed to gradually tilting Britain toward policies like a minimum wage, universal health care and the abolition of private property—he would stand on street corners and lecture to the masses. These days, the common assumption is that alfresco sermonizing is almost entirely done by crazy people. Though that was probably less true in Victorian London, it's still safe to assume that pedestrians wouldn't listen to just anyone. As he later wrote, "pressing people to learn things they do not want to know is as unwholesome and disastrous as feeding them on sawdust." Shaw was quite certain the people wanted to know about his theories, and sure enough, he was very popular.

Now, these ideas may have indeed been perfect for the time, place and audience, but the audience was likely as enthralled with their delivery as their content. In his public speaking, Shaw honed a fine wit for the express purpose of reforming society. There are wits who have lamented the uselessness of talking pretty; Shaw was not one of them. He was a shy young man who, upon realizing oratory could help him get what he wanted, mastered it. Like a stand-up comedian he certainly would have been heckled, so to do his job properly he learned to respond.

At twenty-three, he was dragged to a debating society by a friend. Impressed by the quality of the speaking, he pushed himself to respond. In doing so for the first time, "I suffered agonies that no one suspected. During the speech of the debater I resolved to follow, my heart used to beat as painfully as a recruit's going under fire for the first time. I could not use notes; when I looked at the paper in my hand I could not collect myself enough to decipher a word. And of the four or five wretched points that were my pretext for this ghastly practice of mine, I invariably forgot three—the best three."

He kept at it, determined to make members of the society "reconsider their first impression of me as a discordant idiot." At first, the fire of socialism singed him. Gradually he learned how to use his beliefs to win over a crowd. He also learned how to speak for an hour without notes, mostly by learning everything he could about his chosen subjects and practicing relentlessly.

As he once said, anyone could get his skill for the same price, and a good many people could get it cheaper. Shaw only began his professional writing career at the age of thirty-two. First with music and then with drama, he did something unusual for the time: He wrote reviews that were fun to read. His competition was dull and professorial and he clearly took some pleasure in tweaking their sensibilities by loving what they dismissed (Wagner) and dismissing what they loved (Shakespeare). Wilde said the only thing worse than being talked about is not being talked about; Shaw lived this credo. From criticism, Shaw segued into writing his own plays, and in doing so he created something entirely new on the stage: The shotgun marriage of his righteousness with his wit. A spoonful of sugar helps the medicine go down, and in this case, the mix of the two was precisely tart enough to make him the towering literary figure of his age.

He described this blend of moxie and morality best when it eluded him most. He strongly opposed the First World War and was labeled a German sympathizer for it, but the way he shared these views with a nation at war had him branded a traitor.

"In the right key one can say anything," he wrote to Bertrand Russell at the time. "In the wrong key, nothing: the only delicate part of the job is the establishment of the key."

As his biographer Michael Holroyd notes, "the key was still the same—a combination of immaturity and sophistication, brilliance and prolixity." It just didn't go over very well in wartime England.

This happens pretty much every time a country is in shock; some wit somewhere won't have received the memo from polite society that it's time to turn off the contrarian cleverness—and that's a good thing. By giving everyone else something to get huffy about, they actually help further unite the country in po-faced condemnation. A perfect modern example came on September 12, 2001, when Russell Brand hosted his British MTV show dressed as Osama bin Laden, saying, "Come on guys, get over it. It was yesterday. We've got to move on. We cannot grieve forever." If comedy is tragedy plus time, this removes the time bit. This was the day after, before bin Laden was even officially a suspect. The sheer audacity is enough to make you laugh in spite of yourself.

Similarly, Shaw suggested that those who wanted to destroy Germany should leave the men alone and kill all the women, his idea of a joke. "[O]ne has to learn to laugh at such things in war," he told his sister at the time. As Holroyd writes, "The Shavian wit was like an instinctive snap of detachment that appeared to cut him off from the natural chaos so that he could regard what was going on all round him as already some way past." In other words, he had perspective, objectively a good thing but not necessarily in situations like this.

Thankfully war is not mankind's natural state, and Shaw's habit of looking askew at modern society eventually came back into favor. He did frequently push too far, as with his dream of starting a new phonetic alphabet that would smooth out such wrinkles in the English language as the one that allows the word "wrinkle" to start with a "w" when obviously it ought to be an "r." But more often than not, his wit entertained people, and once he had them in their seats and amused, they would put up with a huge amount of his righteousness.

{ QUIP QUIZ }

1. "You cannot _____
   The motor bus
   And brilliant wit
   Is lost on it."
   —W. J. Turner

2. "_____ is simply the attitude we adopt to people whom we personally dislike."
   —Oscar Wilde

3. "_____ is the most perfect expression of scorn."
   —George Bernard Shaw

4. "You can't teach an old _____ new tricks."
   —Dorothy Parker

5. "Anyone who thinks sitting in church can make you a Christian must also think sitting in your garage can make you a _____."
   —Garrison Keillor

| Cuss | Morality | Silence | Dogma | Car |

Righteousness
WIT LIST

- ☐ MORALIZING + WIT = slightly less annoying moralizing
- ☐ If you're a radical, you must be radically funny
- ☐ Leave the Osama BIN LADEN costume to RUSSELL BRAND

SEVEN

Charm

Featuring: CARY GRANT, TOM HANKS AND
BORIS JOHNSON SMASHING THINGS

◆ ◆ ◆

When it came time to subdivide the six fundamental
building blocks of matter known as quarks, scientists
began with simple directions: "Up" and "down." In what may
have been a moment of self-awareness, they called the third
quark "strange." The final two continued the location theme as
"top" and "bottom," but the fourth was the outlier:
That quark is called "charm."

And there you have as much particle physics
as you'll require to understand wit. (We needn't
dwell on the fact that scientists looking to
isolate the charm quark build special particle
colliders they call charm factories.) Charm can
be found in each and every atom of the universe,
but some of us express it better than others.

In popular culture, any discussion of charm

must begin with Cary Grant. In his best films and in the popular imagination, the actor born (trivia alert!) Archibald Leach always played a character called Cary Grant: Handsome and debonair, sure, but not the least bit concerned with his appearance. He wore the best suits in Hollywood history but never seemed fussy about it. There are no memorable scenes of him checking his look in the mirror, though off screen was another story. Todd McEwen wrote a great essay about how Alfred Hitchcock's *North by Northwest* "isn't a film about what happens to Cary Grant, it's about what happens to his suit." And while calling someone a suit may be an insult, it certainly isn't here. Part of Cary Grant's essence is that he's always perfectly attired. If he ceases to be so, well, he ceases to be Cary Grant. McEwen points out that the film's creepiness comes down to our fears that "in some situation Cary will be inappropriately dressed (Cary GRANT?) and this will hinder him."

To be a leading man in the early days of Hollywood was awkward. As Pauline Kael wrote in her 1975 *New Yorker* profile of Grant, there wasn't much for him to do in his early films, and you can see it on his face. "He became Cary Grant," she writes, "when he learned to project his feelings of absurdity through his characters and to make a style of their feeling silly." Or as Grant put it, "I pretended to be somebody I wanted to be until finally I became that person. Or he became me. Or we met at some point."

Starting from about 1935—basically when he began making the movies we're still watching—he became aware the world around him was faintly ridiculous, and at his best the way he moves, speaks and behaves reflects this. He looks like the knight but acts like the jester. The genius of this was that it gave him all the advantages of being the best-looking guy in the room with none of the drawbacks: As the old line goes, men wanted to be him while women wanted to be with him. As a matinee idol, it's useful if both halves of the traditional couple want to see your new movie.

That's when his charm comes to the fore and when we can see how it fits with his wit. Much of that wit was scripted, so we're really crediting it to Cary Grant the character and not Cary Grant the man, but as we've established, the two Grants are interchangeable. And so it's entirely to his credit that he had alumni of the Algonquin Round Table putting words in his mouth, and that he mouthed them so convincingly.

"Now, it isn't that I don't like you, Susan," he says in *Bringing Up Baby*. "Because, after all, in moments of quiet, I'm strangely drawn to you, but—well, there haven't been any quiet moments."

And as Rosalind Russell hurls her purse at him in *His Girl Friday*, "You're losing your eye. You used to be able to pitch better than that."

Words weren't even necessary. In *The Awful Truth*, the film that made him Cary Grant, he's upstaged by a rival suitor who dances far better than he. Briefly stymied, he watches his girl foxtrot around the floor until he realizes they're putting the chore in choreography. He slips up to the bandleader, offers a small bribe to play the same song again, and returns to his seat to silently and smirkingly watch the other man make a fool of himself by dancing until his legs give out. It's spontaneous, creative, a bit cruel and totally something Cary Grant ought to do.

Grant's Heirs

Cary Grant died in 1986, and though his will didn't specifically bequeath his charm to any one man, the general consensus is that George Clooney inherited it. It helps that they both have a cleft chin. Clooney does have a penchant for practical jokes but he can't quite play George Clooney as well as Grant played Grant. He's great in *Ocean's Eleven*, for instance, though in *Ocean's Twelve* it's a bit too clear that he's fabulously rich and good-looking and your movie ticket helped pay for his place in Lake Como.

Tom Hanks more closely approximates the Cary Grant charm. He's frequently chosen as the most trusted man in America, which is an odd thing given that an actor's job is to pretend to be someone he's not. He's handsome but not aggressively so, meaning he can be a leading man but still fade into the role. (Unlike, say, Brad Pitt, who basically reminds you in every movie that it's Brad Pitt with long hair killing zombies, or Brad Pitt with a mustache killing Nazis, or Brad Pitt in a nice suit bantering with George Clooney.)

But most important, Hanks has the wit. You see it in his talk-show appearances, where he shoots the breeze with a marksman's aim. And when he meets the press, he manages to mock them just gently enough to amuse the smarter people in the room without endangering his Most Trusted Man status. When he was promoting the *Da Vinci Code* movie in Cannes, he was asked, apropos of nothing and presumably by an Icelandic showbiz journalist, why he loved Iceland.

"Why do I love Iceland? We only have a few minutes here," he began, "but I'm just going to start with how sensational the people are. . . . The location is ideal. Summertimes are beautiful. There is a lot of camping and you can get a really great and relatively inexpensive cup of coffee in Iceland."

And to a question about his mullet in the film, he deadpanned: "It's not up to me to decide whether I'm having a bad hair day. I trust the press to communicate that opinion around the world with lightning speed."

But the most charming man in Hollywood, without a doubt, is Robert Downey Jr. As Jeff Bridges famously reported, the first *Iron Man* movie didn't have a script that he was aware of; it was basically just Downey Jr. riffing. His career arc is a Hollywood story in itself: Hyped, self-aware young actor becomes leading man, nearly captures the Oscar but soon after falls into decline, does time, sobers up, figures things out, comes back and coolly cashes in with some of the biggest franchises in motion-picture history. Through it all, he remains erudite and self-aware, only now it's clear that his mildly subversive comments are definitely working for him. His charm essentially consists of Shavian jokes: He just tells the truth, or as much of it as he can get away with. In his business, even a small amount can be a shock. He called his 1996 movie *U.S. Marshals* "probably the worst action movie of all time, and that's just not good for maintaining a good spiritual condition." He did it on *The Tonight Show* in 2013 when he said, "When you're promoting a movie, you go out and, I call it: Grind, monkey, grind." And he did it when he told *GQ*'s Chris Heath that he knew an Oscar would eventually be his: "Look, even if I don't get one directly, eventually they're just going to have to give me one when I get old. So no matter how you slice it, I'm getting one."

But it must be said that these three—even a mulleted Tom Hanks—are all attractive human beings. Does charm require good looks? In theory, it does not. The word itself originally meant a chant or a song, and in Middle English it applied to magicians and their spells. To cast a charm upon one's audience shouldn't require an attractive magician, just a skilled one. To test this, we need to strip away movie-star looks. We need to find a human who looks like a potato and still exudes charm. We need to talk about Boris Johnson.

BaJo Rising

To liken the mayor of London's appearance to a common tuber is barely an insult compared to how the British press describes him on a regular basis. Separated-at-birth photo galleries featuring Boris Johnson alongside monkeys are a staple of newspaper websites. It's not that he's a hugely unattractive man, but rather that he does himself no favors in his dress, actions or demeanor. With his perpetually unkempt hair and penchant for wearing slept-in suits, he's the anti–Cary Grant, composed entirely of Grantimatter. Or to make the much more common comparison, the anti–David Cameron.

Both Johnson and British prime minister Cameron are upper-crust conservative British politicians, both went to Oxford and, perhaps most amusingly, both belonged to that university's notorious Bullingdon Club. This not-so-secret society blends casual wealth with destructive mischief in such a way that reflects poorly on all involved. Most infamously, members will conclude an opulent dinner by savagely trashing the restaurant or club, smashing plates, glasses and windows—and then immediately paying for all the damage and then some in cash. It's hard to imagine a more disgusting display of snobbish entitlement—the alliterative appeal of the phrase "Bullingdon bully" has not been lost on Fleet Street—and the prime minister's opponents have missed no opportunity to hang the name Bullingdon Club around his neck.

To some degree it has stuck to Cameron, but not in any appreciable sense to Johnson. Why is that? In a word, charm. For while at first glance the prime minister is the more Cary Grantish of the two, it's Boris Johnson who appears eminently more comfortable in his own skin. Only his most ardent foe—and more on them in a minute—would accuse him of being anything other than what he is.

Or as Johnson once told the BBC, "As a general tactic in life, it is often useful to give the slight impression that you are deliberately pretending not to know what's going on—because the reality may be that you don't know what's going on, but people won't be able to tell the difference."

And herein lies the key to Johnson's charm, wit and enormous popularity with the voting public: He is tremendously, astonishingly well spoken. It's difficult to think of another public figure in modern times who can compare. Now, when it comes to sweeping rhetoric, yes, Barack Obama is the one who can send shivers up the legs of admiring journalists. But when it comes to actually talking, without a teleprompter and on a subject not of his choosing—in other words, the way you and I have to talk every single day—the U.S. president tends to sound more like the law professor he is by training. He thinks aloud, evaluates various positions, uses plenty of pauses and measured "ahs," and always comes down on the side of nuance.

But when Boris Johnson talks, it's like an expert jazz musician riffing. He finds fully formed epigrams, historical references, comedic intonations, drive-by zingers and verbal jabs in the driest of subjects. He gets himself into trouble much more often than any political consultant would advise, but he either talks his way out of it or simply wins over the public because he is so obviously just being himself.

It must be said that Boris Johnson's charm is just as much a gift from his chromosomes as Cary Grant's: The latter got chiseled features while the inherited a sharp tongue. But there is still much to learn from what the two men share. In both, their charm resides in the obvious fact that they're having fun. Both had the ambition to rise to the heights of their chosen professions; Neither confused ambition with dull earnestness. As Wilde reminds us, life is too important to be taken seriously.

Take, for example, Johnson's line when the 2012 Olympic torch arrived at the Tower of London: "As Henry VIII discovered with at least two of his wives, this is the perfect place to bring an old flame."

Or his riff on Churchill's description of Russia as a "riddle wrapped in an enigma inside a mystery," as he described the rival Liberal Democrat party as a "void within a vacuum surrounded by a great inanition."

As Wilde reminds us, life is too important to be taken seriously.

ZIP POLE

Or his excellent *Daily Telegraph* column upon being demoted as a member of parliament in 2004, which included the final line, "My friends, as I have discovered myself, there are no disasters, only opportunities. And, indeed, opportunities for fresh disasters."

Or the seminal moment of the 2012 London Olympiad, when he tested out a zip line in Victoria Park. In full glare of the world's media, with a baby-blue helmet on, Union Jacks in each hand and his socks showing, he got stuck three quarters of the way down the line. "Can you get me a rope? Get me a rope, OK?" he was heard yelling. As Cameron said with perhaps a tiny tinge of envy, "If any other politician anywhere in the world was stuck on a zip wire, it would be a disaster. For Boris, it's an absolute triumph."

It could be that the secret to his charm lies in the gulf between his verbal fluency and his sartorial sloppiness. No one would be intimidated by unruly hair and a wrinkled suit. Rather, it conveys authenticity—a slick politician, we innately think, looks slick, like Mitt Romney or David Cameron. Someone who can't manage to hide the short end of his tie behind the long end likely isn't trying to hide anything else, this unspoken reasoning goes. When it turns out that he can express himself quite well, it's a mild surprise, but one that conforms to our image of the absentminded professor. And then when he says something blatantly offensive, well, then it can be explained away by a line like "that's just Boris being Boris."

But is being Boris more than an inadvertent combination of shagginess and suavity? As Sonia Purnell, a longtime critic of the London mayor, wrote in the *Observer*, "Former staff reveal how the pauses, the non-sequiturs, the rambling tangents are studiously prepared; the most successful jokes and 'off-the-cuff' Borisisms are rehearsed and recycled." This is quite reminiscent of Churchill's tactics, which makes the main argument of Purnell's column—that he's not prime ministerial material—all the more questionable.

Or to put it with more vitriol, as an Australian writer in the *Guardian* did on the subject of a particularly offensive and apparently offhand (though how can we know?) 2013 Boris line about women needing to go to university to find husbands, "The well-rehearsed, faux-buffoonery of entitled, privately-schooled, Oxford-graduated, conservative male politicians doesn't merely exist as a decoy to the vast social privileges they've enjoyed; it's a deliberate, mocking in-joke towards anyone who was born to less privilege than them." The London mayor's Bullingdon Club past certainly invited that last bit—though describing politicians like Boris as though there's more than one of them is wishful thinking—but the sharpest cut is again the accusation that he's not even a real buffoon!

And as many have shown throughout history, creative spon-

taneity takes practice. In this
particular attack on all the privilege Boris was born into, the
accusation that he is well rehearsed could be taken as a
compliment. He had the intelligence and humility to figure
out what the public wanted from him. It wasn't handed to him
on a silver plate by a white-gloved servant: He worked at it!

Creative spontaneity takes practice.

Indeed, the amazing thing about Boris Johnson's persona is
not that he works at it, it's that it works, period. And if he can
"studiously prepare" to charm the world, there's hope for the rest
of us. Well, maybe not Mitt Romney.

{ QUIP QUIZ }

1. "Everyone wants to be _____. Even I want
   to be _____."   —Cary Grant

2. "All charming people, I fancy, are _____; it is the
   secret of their attraction."   —Oscar Wilde

3. "It is absurd to divide people into good or bad. People
   are either charming or _____."   —Wilde, again

4. "You know what charm is: a way of getting the
   answer _____ without having asked any clear
   question."   —Albert Camus, *La Chute* (1956)

5. "It is a great mistake for men to give up paying compliments, for when they give up saying what is charming, they give up _____ what is charming."

—Wilde, one more time

Cary Grant/ Cary Grant	Spoiled	Tedious	Yes	Thinking

Charm Wit list

☐ Dapper dress*

☐ Dimples (optional)

☐ Be interested in the people and places around you, without being ingratiating

☐ Can you dance?

☐ Hold the door open

* Unless you're going the BOJO route!

EIGHT

Romance

◆ ◆ ◆

There were many lessons to be learned by an adolescent watching *Seinfeld* in the 1990s. Don't make out during *Schindler's List*, for one. Lock your apartment door to keep out the nutty neighbors, for another. But perhaps the biggest take-away, the one so prevalent in Hollywood that it barely seems worth noting, is that all these guys dated way, way out of their league. To be fair, Jerry is a reasonably handsome and successful guy and Kramer wore his eccentricities well. But George? Short, stocky, bald, petty, cheap, dishonest, unemployed, lives with his parents—and consistently dates total knockouts. How does he do it? Is this as fictional as a Manhattan where no one locks their apartment doors? Perhaps. But maybe there's something more to it. George Costanza is a clever guy, especially when he's in his element. When he lies, he lies big. He acknowledges all his faults and still maintains a healthy self-image. And, as you'd expect of a short, stocky bald man with a team of talented writers scripting his every word, he's always got something clever to say.

And therein lies the real-life truth of the sitcom reality: Men with something witty to say to women are naturally going to have more of a chance at striking up a relationship. This is pretty obvious, and to no group more so than the lonely bachelors searching the web for advice on how to be witty. It's safe to say they don't want to channel Churchill; they just want to be able to approach a girl without scaring her off. They want to charm her, sure, but they also want to romance her.

Charm and romance are different degrees of the same attribute. When you set out to charm, you want a great many people to like you. When you set out to romance, you want a much smaller subset to love you. So you recalibrate that wit from a broadcast to a conversation, focusing the interest on one person rather than a roomful. And if it works, then a request for a date should be quickly fulfilled.

The Gender Deride

At this point, we must acknowledge we are talking about lonely guys approaching intimidating girls. Do the gender roles work the other way around? Well, certainly not on network television. But this line of inquiry leads inevitably and unfortunately to that notorious Christopher Hitchens essay entitled "Why Women Aren't Funny." His reasoning is that humor is an evolutionary mechanism developed to encourage procreation and that being a good mother is far too serious a job to allow for laughter. (This was typical of the work of the late provocateur, who was never comfortable being too well-liked or close to mainstream opinion.) This mix of armchair Darwinism, dated generalizations about gender roles, Kipling quotations and logical backflips is as airtight as a Whoopee cushion, and had about the same effect on polite society. Of course women can and do land mates with humor, just as men do so with great hair and high cheekbones. But the essay itself is quite funny, a masterclass in trolling, and deserves to be reread for that reason alone.

One of Hitchens's bold statements that stands up to scrutiny (ours, at least) is that wit is "the unfailing symptom of intelligence." And so its evolutionary function is apparent: The mate who displays wit is intelligent and will thus be more likely than that mate's dumber peers to find hidden stores of food, thwart predators, avoid disease and generally steer clear of misfortune in all its guises. In more prosaic terms, he'll be able to fill life's awkward silences with something worth hearing. This applies to human relationships of all sorts. It also brings us to a modern theory of humor that is central to our understanding of wit as spontaneous creativity.

As we've said before, humor is not wit. But each can make us laugh, and the most convincing theories of why we laugh make plenty of room for both. There's *release theory*, the idea that laughing helps burn off tension that we'd otherwise have to keep bottled up. While this explains nervous giggles, it doesn't do much for wit. *Benign violation theory* has it that we laugh when some social norm is broken, but only in such a way that no real harm is done. This seems true enough but also applies to many things that aren't actually funny. The mean-spirited *superiority theory* basically assumes we're always laughing at you, not with you, and that people only laugh when they believe they're better than you.

Then there's the thesis of Robert Benchley's landmark essay "Why We Laugh—or Do We?": "All laughter is merely a compensatory reflex to take the place of sneezing. What we really want to do is sneeze, but as that is not always possible, we laugh instead." Profound; probably false.

Incongruity-resolution theory is closest to explaining the wit of romance. We are constantly trying to figure out the world around us, and we do so through trial and error: Heading in one direction, realizing it's wrong, backing up and charting a new path, over and over again. A joke simulates this with no consequences beyond not getting it. Why did the hipster burn his tongue?

He drank his espresso before it was cool. Here the parallel tracks of hot coffee and hipsterism converge in a punch line, but you needed to consider both ideas at once and resolve the incongruities.

The final and perhaps most important feature of humor research is that humor research is not at all funny. Time to change the subject.

"Cupid in a Riot"

What to make of Russell Brand, the British comedian, actor and rouser of rabble. With his leather pants, flowing scarves and unkempt hair, he has a look that perfectly fits the rock star Aldous Snow, his character in *Forgetting Sarah Marshall* and *Get Him to the Greek*. British *GQ* declared his look "Evil Gandhi" when they called him the worst-dressed man of 2012, and Brand himself says he's "brilliantly disguised as a scruffbag." Both because of and despite this, he is famously successful with women. As Alec Baldwin, his co-star in the 2012 did-that-actually-happen Tom Cruise hair-metal musical *Rock of Ages*, explained to *The Hollywood Reporter*, Brand has "magical powers. . . . When Russell would come on set, all the women were adjusting their tops and hair."

He calls himself "hysterically heterosexual" and has thoroughly documented his urges and their resolution in two bestselling volumes of memoir, aptly titled *My Booky Wook* and *Booky Wook 2*. In that sense, the sex just seems like another manifestation of his constant need for attention. Watch his comedy special, send him hate mail, spend the night: All of it has different degrees of the same effect on him. The applause of a roomful of people gives him a high, as do the attentions of a bedful. As he notes at one point, he's looking for "sex or applause," and there doesn't seem to be much of a preference.

Brand is a great case study for the fact that wit is amoral. Just as the force of gravity will equally help a bridesmaid catch a bouquet and a seagull besmirch a freshly washed car, the power of spontaneous creativity can both propagate noble ideas and louche intentions. It's a tool, just as, sometimes, so is he.

His signature move is an eloquent digression delivered in an unexpected venue. As he makes his living as a celebrity, this means just about anywhere he goes is an unexpected venue for eloquence. At its best, this has the effect of turning the attention away from himself and onto the ridiculousness of stardom itself. After his breakup with singer Katy Perry, for instance, an entertainment reporter asked him an innocuous and moderately dumb question about how he was holding up.

"Quite well, thank you. Are you asking because of recent events?" he replied. "Well I suppose what you're doing is you're making the mistake of seeing time as linear. The brilliant American author Kurt Vonnegut, he'll tell you that if you imagine reality as experienced simultaneously, events become redundant. . . . I don't want to further celebrate the overly elaborate, brittle plastic structures of nonsense that are constantly fired into our minds to distract us from what's really important. So if I'd done something actually newsworthy . . . then I'd cover it. But if it was just more lacquered nonsense, designed to distract us from truth, then I would wisely ignore it."

And then there was his 2013 appearance on MSNBC's *Morning Joe*, on which he mercilessly mocked the morning-show hosts, which was quite funny if a little unfair. He was appearing, after all, on the lacquered nonsense section of the show reserved for comedians promoting their tours. That morning, he acknowledged the essential rudeness of staged interviews by pointing out that the hosts were talking about him while he was right there in the studio.

"You are talking about me as if I'm not here and as if I'm an extraterrestrial," he says. "You know I'm from a country that is near to you."

He also directed some crude innuendo toward Mika Brzezinski, who did seem unduly flustered by Brand's physical presence.

"That's the problem with current affairs," Brand says. "You forget about what's important. You allow the agenda to be decided by superficial information. What am I saying? What am I talking about? Don't think about what I'm wearing. These things are redundant, they're superficial."

"I'm distracted by—" Brzezinski mumbles.

"Don't be distracted! What do you think that gesture means, the way you're grasping that bottle? What does that indicate? What's the subtext in that? You need to lose that ring, Mika, it don't mean nothing to ya. She's grasping at shafts! She's a shaft grasper!"

This call for higher debate followed by some sexualized teasing of his interviewer is, shall we say, not internally coherent. Many would find it distasteful. But two things are undeniable: He's being spontaneously creative, and he ably directs this toward women he deems receptive.

So where did he get his wit? Many of the great British wits of recent times—Wilde, Stoppard, Amis, Hitchens, Johnson—seemed to have found theirs at Oxford or Cambridge, just as many of their American counterparts worked at the *Harvard Lampoon*. It's as if they spent their time in the ivory tower having high-minded conversations laden with literary and historical allusions, and then didn't let the fact they'd graduated stop them. Or rather, their entry into London intellectual life was essentially seamless.

Brand certainly wasn't that. He did briefly attend Drama Centre London, a fairly prestigious acting school where he would have learned his Shakespeare. But he was drunk for most of his time there—in fact, he was drunk during his audition—so it seems unlikely that much of it stuck. Rather, he appears to be an autodidact. He describes taping and listening to his stand-up comedy routines over and over again, studying the patterns for clues as to how to do it better. As he said of the show *Vic Reeves Big Night Out*: "It taught me that you should never pick the first word people would think of, you have to train your mind to sift through the obvious stuff until you come to something that's really funny." For proof of this, think of *Spy* magazine's famous 1980s description of Donald Trump as a "thick-fingered vulgarian." Sure, you could make fun of his hair, his opinions or his business acumen, but those are all the obvious targets. His pudgy digits, be they real or metaphorical, are much better objects of ridicule.

And then there's the Hitchensesque descriptions of being on television: "I have this feeling when I'm on TV that I'm resting,"

Brand says. The total adoration of the spotlight—to the point that he seems uncomfortable when it's not on him—is a powerful and unhealthy motivation to come up with material.

How did he get this way? His *Booky Wooks*, with every conquest and failed attempt exhaustively detailed, offer extensive background. His father was a lothario who withheld approval, while his mother smothered her son, and he, her. So when he explains how one of his father's grandest gestures toward his only son was a sex tour of Thailand, or when he titles a chapter "Mummy Helen" and explains how the presence of actress Helen Mirren blazes "right to the writhing uterus of my throbbing Oedipus complex," well, there's no need to guess at what he's trying to say.

As he puts it in his first book:

Socrates says the male libido is like being chained to a madman, and the links in my chain are these:

1. I love sex, like everyone, because of the ol' biological program.

2. I enforce my identity and status as a man through sex and the seduction of women. And:

3. I have a hopelessly addictive nature.

Point one is scientific fact. Point two would alternately disgust or sadden many right-thinking people, but he's voicing an uncomfortable truth about sex and power. (In a similar vein is his observation about the phrase "make people laugh." As he writes, "I even love the idiom—there's no choice. The person making them do it has the power.")

And point three is perhaps the saddest part of the two books and subsequent public life of Russell Brand. That's because the first book is written from the perspective of a patient at a sexual addiction treatment center, where Brand is dealing with the fact that he is "on the brink of becoming sufficiently well known for my carnal overindulgences to cause me professional difficulties," and the second book, published three years later, begins with an entire chapter about how he came to sleep with Kate Moss. (In short: He couldn't believe it was happening, was shocked by "the chaos she has left in my belly" and, most important for him, knew it would make him really, truly famous. And she made the bed.) The second book ends with his engagement to Katy Perry.

"From the first date I changed," he says of his wife-to-be. "No more women. Well, actually, thousands of women. I wake up to a different one each day, but they're all her." Their marriage lasted fourteen months, but if nothing else it provided a redemptive end to *Booky Wook 2* and a potential beginning for *Booky Wook 3*.

The most interesting thing about his time with Perry, for our purposes, was their courtship. He pursued her with the quips and suggestive comments that comprise the Brand wit—and she replied in kind in a sequence he describes like a romantic comedy.

"I'm a sorcerer with the birds, an alchemist," he's telling an assembled crowd. "You put a dame in front of me and I will hypnotize her with my sheer magne—" and at this point, Perry throws a (presumably plastic) bottle at his head, hitting him like "Cupid in a riot." (or like Rosalind Russell with better aim.)

She points out that his big head and ridiculous hair make an easy target. He thinks, *Wit don't fail me now*, and weakly observes that she's wearing sunglasses indoors, which explains her ridiculous choice of sweaters. She says it's hard to take fashion advice "from a man who looks like a lazy transvestite." He counters that next to her, he does look feminine, and demands she take off her sunglasses. She refuses to "take off anything I'm wearing around you, I could get herpes."

This back-and-forth fits nicely into the rich history of screwball comedies featuring women who give as good as they get, from *His Girl Friday* to *Moonlighting*. If the courtly love tradition features the lute-playing suitor serenading his mute beloved with syrupy sentiments, this is its modern equivalent: A gentle insult was much more effective than comparing thee to a summer's day. In Brand's words—used to describe seducing not one but two reluctant women—"if you can unpick the social stitching with some beautifully put universal truths, a good time can be had by all."

Pluck Be a Lady

At this point, the use of romantic wit as a seduction tool may seem like an exclusively male domain. The less attractive man woos the more attractive woman by closing the gap with his clever words. That's the tradition that's been part of Western culture for hundreds of years.

But consider how a woman described by her own biographer as "a somewhat dumpy, short and almost nondescript figure"—a veritable female George Costanza—became the ultimate sex symbol of the early screen. Mae West might have been fairly ordinary in appearance, but her mastery of the double entendre and her facility with a knowing wink made her for a time the world's most desired woman.

She did this with practically no love scenes in her movies; a few chaste kisses were about all that were permitted. All the foreplay was wordplay and she was an expert at twisting it to her ends. Furthermore, she got away with it because it was both funny and outrageous: An outright statement of her innuendo would have certainly been banned. And in most cases, it was West doing the implying: Unlike Cary Grant, many of her most famous lines were hers alone. They weren't in the script and weren't so much ad-libbed as studiously prepared. Trained on the vaudeville stage like Groucho Marx and W. C. Fields, she was used to intense rehearsals. In this way, it's fair to say one of the great sex symbols in motion picture history was not Mae West's body but her mind.

Like many of the Great Wits, her reputation was self-sustaining. In the film *I'm No Angel*, nearly every line was taken to have a double meaning. "Oh Beulah, peel me a grape," her character calls out to a servant, an ad-libbed reference taken to be mysteriously sexual but actually intended to describe something West's pet monkey, Beulah, could do. "When I'm good, I'm very good, but when I'm bad, I'm better," comes from the same film, as does her description of herself as a woman who "climbs the ladder of success wrong by wrong." She would often complain that "people seem to read double meanings into every word I speak," but this was a slippery statement on its own. Sometimes she put them there, and on occasion, perhaps, she didn't.

To wit, in 1933's *She Done Him Wrong*, there was, "Why don't you come up sometime and see me?"—later twisted to the more mellifluous "come up and see me sometime" and universally understood as a carnal invitation. As well as, "when women go wrong, men go right after." And when it's suggested men would be safer if she were in handcuffs: "Oh, I don't know—hands ain't everything."

"Haven't you ever met a man who makes you happy?" her character is asked in the same film, to which she replies, "Sure. Lots of times."

After the 1937 to 1938 success of Walt Disney's first animated feature: "I used to be Snow White, but I drifted."

To a policeman in the 1930s, the immortal: "Is that a pistol in your pocket or are you just happy to see me?"

And in a 1960 appearance on Red Skelton's variety show, when asked to describe some of the offbeat men in her past, she responded, "Well, a smart girl never beats off any man."

Her real wit was all suggestion: Allowing the audience to connect dots the censors couldn't see, and letting them know she approved. It was simultaneously crass, refined and unique. They were often but not always double entendres, so better to coin a new term for a Mae Westism: The trouble entendre. To give her the last word: "It's not what I do, but the way I do it. It's not what I say, but the way I say it."

{ QUIP QUIZ }

1. "The only real argument for _____ is that it remains the best method for getting acquainted."

—Heywood Broun

2. "If it weren't for _____, I'd have no sex life at all."

—Rodney Dangerfield

3. "I thought I was _____ but it turns out I was just thorough."

—Russell Brand

4. "Summer bachelors, like summer _____, are never as cool as they pretend to be."

—Nora Ephron

5. "DNA rhymes with _____."

—George Murray

Marriage	Pickpockets	Promiscuous	Breezes	1 & A

Romance
Wit list

- [ ] If you're not pretty,
  make sure to be witty
- [ ] Pick the adjective
  less traveled
- [ ] Entendre
- [ ] Entendre

NINE

Resilience

Featuring: The wit of both the "The Jerk Store" and staircase, Al Jaffee, Nora Ephron, Mark Twain and the moment Groucho Marx decided to throw out the script

◆ ◆ ◆

Denis Diderot was at a Paris dinner party when a friend shocked him with a pointed remark about two famed writers of the day.

"This riposte disconcerts me and reduced me to silence, because a sensitive man like myself becomes so wrapped up in his objection to the argument that he loses his head, and he doesn't find it again until he's at the bottom of the stairs," Diderot later wrote in his eighteenth-century essay "Paradoxe sur le Comédien."

"Another man, cold-minded and master of himself, would have replied—" and then he proceeds to enumerate a lengthy response.

Flash-forward about two hundred years. The management team of the New York Yankees is talking before a table filled with food in a boardroom. Most members have a few small items on their plates, with the exception of the team's traveling secretary.

This man is stuffing his face with shrimp, taking one after another, barely stopping to chew them. With a complete lack of self-awareness and his mouth full of seafood, he chimes in to his colleagues' conversation.

"Hey, George, the ocean called," Reilly replies. "They're running out of shrimp."

This is of course "The Comeback" episode of *Seinfeld*, more commonly known as "The Jerk Store" for the riposte George Costanza comes up with in the next scene, as he's driving home from work: "Oh yeah? Well, the jerk store called, and they're running out of you!"

"Riposte" means "retort" in French, and in fencing it's how you respond to an attack. Your opponent attacks and you parry, or block that attack with your blade. The riposte is the immediate counterattack. In both swordplay and wordplay, there's something deeply satisfying about it. The very definition of the word asserts your innocence; you were attacked! We aren't told if you did anything to deserve it but we can give you the benefit of the doubt. You were just standing there in your ridiculous white fencing uniform when someone lunged at you!

In response, you block the attack—hooray!—and rather than engage in some namby-pamby nonaggression pact, you immediately hit back. Any fair-minded observer would not only admit you were justified in doing do; he or she would also probably be rooting for you. You took a hit and barely flinched before retaliating. Well done.

Unless, of course, you didn't. In their respective times and places, Diderot and Costanza experienced a phenomenon that has frustrated humans for as long as we've been able to talk to each other: Coming up with the perfect reply long after the window to use it has closed. The French term, from Diderot, is *"l'esprit d'escalier,"* which directly translates as "the wit of the staircase" but can now be rendered as "the jerk store." (Interestingly, the German translation of *"l'esprit d'escalier,"* *"treppenwitz,"* used to mean "a comeback that comes too late" but over the years has come to mean "a bad joke that seemed funny at the time.")

All of which is fascinating from a theoretical perspective but not much use when you're the guy who's just been zinged for your mouthful of shrimp. Then what do you do?

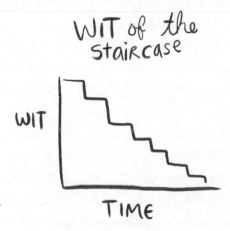

The Snappiest Answerer

Among his many contributions to modern culture, Al Jaffee attempted to solve this problem. Jaffee was a charter member of the Usual Gang of Idiots, which is not an insult but in fact high praise: He was one of the artists who made *Mad* magazine an institution.

He's best known for "Fold-Ins," those back-page cartoons that would reveal a hidden joke when twice folded vertically. Seasoned readers could decode them without creasing their magazines, thereby saving themselves some manual labor and developing neural pathways of little to no use in other endeavors.

That alone would be enough for most Idiots, but Jaffee also came up with the long-running gag strip called "Snappy Answers to Stupid Questions." He has frequently explained its origins in public appearances, always dating it back to when he lived on Long Island and would routinely have to climb onto the roof of his house to straighten the television antenna.

"I'd have to borrow a ladder and climb up, though I'm terrified of heights, and straighten the antenna," he recalled in a 2011 appearance. "One day I'm up there and I heard footsteps on the ladder behind me, and the footsteps arrive closer, and it's my son, who says, 'Where's Mom?' And, you know, I'm clinging for dear life, and I said, 'I've killed her and I'm stuffing her down the chimney.' Two benefits resulted from this: One was that I was able to create a number of books based on 'Snappy Answers,' and the other is that my son stopped talking to me."

By this account, it would seem some combination of fear and adrenaline was responsible for the senior Jaffee's snide remark. But since we are rarely in that agitated state when confronted with a Stupid Question, his cartoons acted as a sort of study guide to get the better of inquisitive fools. Typically, they'd feature one question along the lines of: Is that your dog?

To which the person holding a dog might reply:

A. No, this is my neighbor's dog. My dog is in my neighbor's lap!

B. No, it's my wife Selma showing her appreciation for the fur coat I bought her.

C. No, it's a hairy hot-water bottle!

D. Fill in your own Snappy Answer.

These were a minor sensation in the 1970s, which Jaffee happily and avidly milked for as long as he could. He dedicated the second book of "Snappy Answers" to "The people at *Mad* who made it possible, and the people at the IRS who made it necessary!" and the fourth begins with a "tearful lament" by fellow Idiot Jerry DeFuccio begging him in rhyme to stop spewing out the collections. The first two books sold more than two million copies, and in total the series ran for eight volumes. "I can't come up with blockbuster ideas all the time," Jaffee told his biographer, "so I cheat by repeating myself."

To keep the franchise going, he extended it to include "Stinging Comebacks to Snappy Answers to Stupid Questions" (Cabbie: "Want a taxi?" Pedestrian: "No, I'm frantically waving my hands like this to attract a water buffalo." Cabbie: "Don't worry . . . with your face and figure you can't miss!") as well as the virtually identical category of "Snappy Answers to Stupid Questions That Backfired" (Cop: "Did he grab your pocketbook?"

Victim: "No, it jumped into his hands by itself!" Cop: "Goody! Looks better on him than you!").

In a way, even his "Fold-Ins" were Snappy Comebacks: He's said they were his version of the centerfolds that were making *Playboy* famous in the 1950s, except instead of folding out they went in the opposite direction.

Were any of Al Jaffee's Snappy Comebacks ever successfully deployed? It seems unlikely, as even the best of them has a certain *Mad* sensibility that wouldn't make much sense in a world where people don't react to Borscht Belt witticisms by leaping into the air with shock lines haloing their heads. But the long-running feature and the books it spawned at least planted the seed in adolescent minds across the English-speaking world: When someone says something stupid to you, it's a good idea to have a snappy comeback at the ready. We all know what to do when life gives you lemons, but it feels even better to throw a lemon right back. You want to be resilient—to hold your own, to turn a sour moment into your own sweet revenge.

Jaffee's early life is a greater testament to resilience, and a greater cosmic joke than anything he ever submitted to *Mad*. A Lithuanian Jew, he was born in Savannah, Georgia, in 1921—but his unstable mother abducted him and his siblings to return to the Baltic shtetl, essentially living a peasant's life from the previous century. Al took refuge in the comics sent by his distraught father and figured out how to survive with a neglectful and occasionally abusive mother.

"I became aware that I could not trust adults," he tells Mary-Lou Weisman in her 2010 biography, *Al Jaffee's Mad Life*. "My father let me be schlepped to Europe; my mother did the schlepping. . . . I developed my own brand of anti-adultism. At an early age, I set out to prove that adults were full of shit."

As Weisman writes, when Jaffee looks at a newspaper, he sees "bullshit—adults behaving like silly, pompous hypocrites, always asking stupid questions. Making fun of them is Al's best revenge."

Eventually, in 1933, Jaffee's father managed to convince his mother that, with Hitler in power in Germany and parts of Lithuania becoming parts of Poland, it was time to send the children back to the United States. (Well, most of them: Al and two of his brothers returned, while his mother's favorite stayed behind until 1940, when he was finally sent to safety. Mildred Jaffee was most likely murdered by either Nazis or Lithuanian partisans in 1941.)

Al Jaffee's talent for drawing, spurred by the comics he would pore over, gained him acceptance to the newly formed Fiorello H. LaGuardia High School of Music and Art. There he met Will Elder and Harvey Kurtzman, and thirteen years later the three cartoonists would be among the creators of *Mad* magazine.

Jaffee's career careened through ups and downs, but at *Mad* he eventually established his place, one he would occupy for decades. He was perpetually the anti-adult, even as an octogenarian. As a child he suffered the foolish actions of grown-ups; as a grown-up he no longer suffered fools. They asked stupid questions; he supplied snappy comebacks to millions of irritated children. His childhood of poverty and starvation cemented his role as the adolescent's advocate, the cartoonist who would help his readers endure the idiocy of the adult world.

Bouncing Back and Then Some

Nora Ephron famously married a man who "was capable of having sex with a Venetian blind." The fact that we know this is a testament to her resilience. Confronted with the dissolution of her marriage, the writer turned it into *Heartburn* and ended up being played by Meryl Streep in the movie. From this—and concurrent with her writing the much more serious film *Silkwood*—she vaulted into Hollywood as a screenwriter and director. When she died in 2012 at the age of seventy-one, she was remembered for many things—Meg Ryan's orgasm scene in *When Harry Met Sally*, feeling bad about her breasts in a 1972 *Esquire* piece and about her neck in a 2006 book, her brand of winking feminism—but never as a wronged woman. When her second marriage was mentioned, it was always to illustrate how she had used the setback to advance her life and career.

Ephron, in the 1960s and 1970s, was a prodigious journalist known for quick copy and quicker wit. In marrying Carl Bernstein, she had paired with one of the most famous journalists of her time, half of the team that brought down Nixon, the half played by Dustin Hoffman in the movie.

He was also playing around, having an affair with Margaret Jay, wife of the former British ambassador. This was really the critical point in Ephron's life, the time when all the snappy writing translated into action. She was clever and sharp, but how would that fit with being the spurned wife?

It fit terrifically, for everyone but Bernstein. As her screenwriter parents always reminded her, both in words and deeds, everything is copy. And furthermore, she had been "raised to know that all painful things eventually turn into funny stories." So she turned the whole story of her marriage to Bernstein into the novel *Heartburn*. This, as she said later, was not something women were supposed to do in 1982. "You were just supposed to curl up into a ball and move to Connecticut," she recalled in a 2007 interview.

The whole point of *Heartburn*, the part that her career and her legacy reveals to be true, is a lesson she imparts in that same 2007 interview: "If you slip on a banana peel, people laugh at you, but if you tell people you slipped on a banana peel, it's your joke, and you're the hero of the joke. It basically is the greatest lesson I think you can ever give anyone."

The events of *Heartburn* were in many ways the ultimate test of that advice, because her extremely public split was a banana-peel slip that left all of Washington laughing at her, but her novel and movie had the entire nation laughing—or crying, or at the very least empathizing—at her joke. She refused to be a victim and instead pushed the banana peel advice to the biggest stage she could, and it worked.

Or as Heather Havrilesky put it in a *Bookforum* review of the posthumous essay collection *The Most of Nora Ephron*, "When life gave Ephron lemons, in other words, she made a vat of really good vodka-spiked lemonade and invited all of her friends and her friends' friends over to share it, and gossip, and play charades."

Dealing with Slights the Mark Twain Way

If Al Jaffee threw life's lemons back and Nora Ephron made vodka lemonade from them, then Mark Twain created something like artisanal *limoncello* from the citric insults of existence. That is to say, he would take the irritant of the moment and laboriously distill it to a lasting truth.

The best aphorisms, when read, always sound like they were just tossed off. The ones that come with an origin story usually stress this point; it was an impromptu dare to use the word "horticulture" in a sentence that allegedly prompted Dorothy Parker to blurt, "You can lead a horticulture but you can't make her think." If the background had been that she'd thought of that while at her writing desk, it wouldn't be nearly as good. Which is why it's comforting to read a particularly nice description of the process involved in distilling pith in Mark Twain's *Autobiography*.

In 1907, while on board a ship to Bermuda, Twain experienced "an incident of a sort which always troubles me, grieves me, and makes me weary of life and long to lie down in the peaceful grave and be at rest." He doesn't give specifics, but think for a moment, if you can, of some occurrence in your life that you might describe in these terms. A boorish person, for instance, or a humiliating turn of events. What was your coping strategy? Chances are it was not Twain's.

"Such incidents usually move me to try to find relief in the building of a maxim," he writes. The goal is to "get the venom out of yourself and into the maxim." But, he warns in a comforting admission, maxims are "not easy to make; they do not come in right shape at the first call; they are creatures of evolution, of development; you have to try several plans before you get one that suits you, or even fairly close to suiting you."

He then proceeds to coin four variations on the theme of, if you laugh at your own joke, it isn't really that funny. "When you laugh at your own funny things you are asking alms for their poverty" is his best crack at it, but he quickly admits it isn't up to his standards.

"The relief is not perfect, but it will have to do," he writes. "I do not feel as axiomatic as usual to-day."

The important point here is that even one of the greatest wits of his time both worked at it and had off days. A secondary and interesting idea is axiom building as therapy. When something significant happens to you, can you craft it into a concise and memorable life lesson? If so, does it get the venom out? Even if you never try this, it sheds new light upon all sorts of aphorisms. When Wilde said, "There is only one thing in the world worse than being talked about, and that is not being talked about," for instance, we can look beyond the wisdom and imagine the original bit of gossip, the hurt it caused, and the eventual and much longer lasting epigram they combined to create. It's worth remembering that the speakers of these famous lines spoke them for reasons beyond giving us something to quote. They choked on grains of sand and coughed up pearls of, if not wisdom, then at least memorable phrasing.

The Inflection Point of Groucho Marx

When we look back at legendary figures in history, it's hard to remember that they wouldn't have known they were legends during most of their lifetimes. That they'd become those we now revere required a combination of talent, perseverance, luck and, most of all, resilience.

In many cases, it's the transition between acts in the play of life that's both most important and most unlikely. Churchill between the wars was pretty much washed up, for instance, and his triumph as wartime prime minister would have seemed a joke to his contemporaries just a few years earlier. There's something to be said for being written off as yesterday's man, for if you can overcome that stigma, you're likely also able to avoid yesterday's problems. And for sheer memorability, racking up notable achievements at different stages of your life gives the general impression that you've always been around—an important first step to becoming a legend.

Making these transitions between life's acts can take years or even decades. Or, as in the case of Groucho Marx, it can take a matter of minutes.

Chico, Harpo, Zeppo, Gummo and Groucho began life as Leonard, Adolph, Herbert, Milton and Julius Marx. They triumphed in vaudeville and used their skills to jump to the movies, becoming the first to use test audiences to refine their films. Working with Irving Thalberg at MGM, they toured films like *A Night at the Opera* and *A Day at the Races*, cutting the bad jokes and adding better ones until they had surefire crowd pleasers.

But by 1947, it looked like Groucho Marx's career was over. He'd had an amazing run, first in vaudeville and then in the movies, but the Marx Brothers had lowercased their B, as it were, and he was now a solo act who didn't quite fit into modern show business.

In March of that year, he was offered a small part in a radio special hosted by Bob Hope. As his son, Arthur, later wrote, "A steady job would have been better, but he readily consented to do this one show anyway."

Groucho had never been completely at ease in radio and the script he had in front of him didn't threaten to change that fact. He was in the middle of the bill and came on late in the show.

"Ordinarily my father is not a comic who becomes annoyed when other comics are getting laughs," Arthur wrote. "But while he waited for his first cue, he somehow got the notion that he was being overshadowed by Hope's performance, and the idea made him furious."

Had Marx stuck to the script, it's likely he would have continued his slow drift down the playbill, from midlist to a black-and-white curio in the television age. Fortunately and perhaps angrily, he improvised—and even more fortunately, Hope played along.

In the skit, he and Hope were supposed to be in a desert, and so Hope opened with the line, "Well, Groucho Marx! Groucho, what are you doing out here in the desert?"

To which Marx replied, "Heh heh"—a chuckle that seems to indicate his decision to go for it—"Desert? I've been sitting in the dressing room for 40 minutes. Some desert, all right."

They then return to the script:

"Selling mink coats, and here's the beauty, only $40."

"Mink coats for $40? How can you sell them so cheap?"

"Well, I have no overhead, I don't advertise, I don't pay rent and I steal the coats."

"Groucho! I know you don't steal those coats, so where'd you get 'em?"

"Very simple, I trap them with my big musical trap. I walk out into the woods and play seductive music on my zither. The little animals hear the music, do a striptease and take off their furs."

"Did I tell you about the two vultures who were plucking each other—" Hope begins.

"Well, it's hard to do without two," Marx responds, suggestively stretching a simple rhyme.

Recognizing genius, Hope breaks character to shout, "You can start working on the record now, fellas."

Later in the skit, as the two men are supposed to be walking into the studio, Marx again breaks character by pointing out the hackneyed sound effects with the remark, "Notice everybody in radio wears wooden shoes?" And then, during one labored audio simulation of a boxing match, Marx again makes jokes at the expense of his jokes. "It's a nice part I've got here, eh? Now wait till I get this line out: 'Hey Hope, what is this?'"

The audience loved the whole exchange, which went on much longer than was necessary for *The Walgreen Hour*. One particularly impressed audience member was John Guedel, a radio and television producer who saw just what he was looking for in Groucho Marx.

"Hiring you to do a show in which you read the script is like buying a Cadillac limousine to haul coal," he told Marx. Guedel offered him the quiz show *You Bet Your Life*, which prompted a similar flight of metaphor from *Newsweek*'s critic, who claimed that using a talent like Marx's for a trendy but insignificant game show was like "selling [champion racehorse] Citation to the glue factory."

But they missed the point, as *You Bet Your Life* wasn't about the game at all. It was really about Marx's wit, plain and simple. As he explained to his daughter in a letter, "apparently the quality of ad libbing on the air is so low that if anyone comes along with even a moderately fresh note he's considered practically a genius."

He'd be introduced to contestants and the one-liners would quickly follow—though in the style that has become standard on all talk shows, Groucho knew many of their details ahead of time. The show was filmed in a single one-hour take, with cameras rolling from every angle and all eyes on the host and his spontaneity. The banter essentially came in two flavors: jeers and leers. The first were his generic quips upon learning of his contestants' occupations.

To a cartoonist: "If you want to see a comic strip, you should see me in a shower."

To an admiral: "We're not very formal on the show, so do you mind if I call you captain?"

To a tree surgeon: "Have you ever fallen out of a patient?"

And the second type were directed to young female contestants and accompanied with a waggle of the famous Groucho eyebrows.

"You have a very good head on your shoulders, and I wish it were on mine."

"Your father is a meat distributor? Well, if you're any indication, he certainly knows his business."

"Would you like to join me for moon gazing some night when there isn't any moon?"

You Bet Your Life ran until 1961 and then went into syndication through the 1970s. It introduced Marx to a whole new generation of fans and reinvented a vaudeville star for the television age. This was an exceptionally rare feat, one largely made possible by the fact that Groucho Marx's wit was timeless—as Woody Allen, possibly his biggest fan, has said, "He is simply unique in the same way that Picasso or Stravinsky are and I believe his outrageous unsentimental disregard for order will be equally funny a thousand years from now. In addition to all this, he makes me laugh."

But this talent alone wouldn't have continued his career much past his final movies. It was Groucho Marx's resilience, the marshaling of his wit to fight for the acclaim he deserved (and, it must be said, a fair stroke of luck), that secured his reinvention as a comic legend.

{ QUIP QUIZ }

1. "The trouble with staging a _____ is the position you come back to." —George Murray

2. "_____: What a person thinks of after he has become a departee." Dan Bennett

3. "Angels can fly because they take themselves _____." —G. K. Chesterton

4. "An escalator can never break. It can only become _____." —Mitch Hedberg

5. "We are all worms. But I do believe I am a _____."

   —Winston Churchill

| Comeback | Repartee | Lightly | Stairs | Glowworm |

RESILIENCE
WIT LIST

- ☐ If you are plagued by the wit of the staircase, take the elevator
- ☐ If life throws you lemons, make something less obvious than lemonade
- ☐ go away
- ☐ come back

TEN

Compassion

Featuring: HEY WAIT: COMPASSION? IS THAT A TYPO?
DON'T YOU MEAN CRUELTY? ANSWER: NO. WIT CUTS BOTH WAYS,
AND WE'RE GONNA GIVE THIS ONE TO THE GOOD GUYS.

◆ ◆ ◆

Way back at the beginning of this book, we considered some of the reasons wit may have fallen out of favor. There was the problem of its definition, which had grown to encompass everything from humor to wisdom. There was the idea that the word "creativity" had taken the place of its most useful meaning. And there was the possibility that something best displayed in ad hoc conversation could never be preserved long enough to sustain our interest.

All of these explanations are well and good, but now we must turn to the nastiest theory: Wit is too mean for our time.

For immediate confirmation of this, we need merely lug Kenneth McLeish's ponderous *Key Ideas in Human Thought* down from the reference shelf and flip to the "W"s. There, we learn that in the English-speaking world, witty people "tend to be regarded as dangerous, to be admired rather than loved (at least in the way that humorous people are loved), and so that self-depreciation (irony against oneself) is the only really favored form."

In addition to throwing that even-more-misused word "irony" in the mix, this observation seems downright bleak. With our definition of wit as spontaneous creativity, it can certainly lead to humor but doesn't have to, and there's no sense putting it up against humor. But many have done so and found them to be diametrically opposed. The critic John Simon argues that they are in fact opposites: In his view, humor is "basically good natured and often directed toward oneself," while wit is "aggressive, often destructive (though one hopes, in a good cause), and almost always directed at others." This takes the old definition of wit as a rapid assemblage of disparate ideas but adds, perhaps, the proviso that when you strike the ideas together, you create a spark that burns somebody. A pratfall on a banana peel garners a laugh but little more; a witty jibe gets the guffaw but leaves the listener with something more substantial.

Charles S. Brooks's essay "On the Difference between Wit and Humor" made a similar point in 1919, and came firmly down on the side of humor. He unleashes a series of analogies and metaphors just tiresome enough to earn his essay a place in high school anthologies. "If a humorous person falls out of a canoe he knows the exquisite jest while his head is still bobbing in the cold water," he wrote. "A witty man, on the contrary, is sour until he is changed and dry: but in a week's time when company is about, he will make a comic story of it." In other words, the humorous man is a fool, whereas the wit has both a survival instinct and the ability to laugh at himself.

Brooks further observed that: "Wit is a lean creature with sharp inquiring nose, whereas humor has a kindly eye and comfortable girth. Wit, if it be necessary, uses malice to score a point—like a cat it is quick to jump—but humor keeps the peace in an easy chair."

If humor is fat and lethargic while wit is agile and sharp, again, it seems a no brainer. All of these arguments are faulty, though, because they reduce wit to a sort of clever nastiness. But Tom Stoppard isn't nasty, nor is Mark Twain. All of the wits in this book have their sharp edges, but what's life without edge? Wit is the thought process that generates truly funny observations, as well as the most incisive comments, lasting quips and brilliant asides. To say wit is mean is like saying the sun is mean for burning you: The giant ball of hot plasma at the center of our solar system is bigger than that, and why weren't you wearing sunscreen in the first place?

Cruel Wit, Bleeding into Snark

All that said, we can turn to the thing known as cruel wit. Our definition doesn't preclude this: One can certainly use spontaneous creativity to make others suffer. In such instances, wit seems more like a social weapon than a grace, a sharp tool used not to repair but to damage.

Take, for example, the times Ricky Gervais hosted the Golden Globes. The traditional job of the awards show host is to throw out jokes about the stars that make a plastic knife seem deadly. The targets, suffering nary a scrape, can then provide knowing laughter for the reaction shot to show what good sports they are. Everyone in Hollywood stays the best of friends while the viewers at home drift off to sleep.

Gervais brought out the machete and the resulting bloodshed made the show worth watching. The jokes were really just observations you wouldn't make in polite company and certainly not if you were the host—certain stars had substance abuse problems; the Hollywood Foreign Press Association is at or slightly below repute; not all the nominated movies were, in fact, good.

The act and its reception revealed a cultural divide between England and the United States. The British, as the *Economist* wrote after Gervais's second stint as Globes host, have a unique appetite for teasing, irreverence and mean-spirited jokes. "Anyone from anywhere can be cruel, anyone from anywhere can be witty, but there is something particularly British about cruel wit," the British magazine opined, citing Evelyn Waugh, A. A. Gill and John Lennon. Yes, the same John Lennon who imagined all the people sharing all the world also forever slighted Ringo Starr with the observation that not only was he not the best drummer in said world, he wasn't even the best drummer in the Beatles. (Ringo wore the slight well, and in his 2003 book of collected postcards, he included one from Paul McCartney that read, "You are the greatest drummer in the world. Really.")

Cruel people can deploy wit as a weapon, but that says more about them than wit. Waugh was so full of bile it eventually dissolved him. As Christopher Hitchens succinctly described the British novelist, "Waugh was a celebrated misanthrope and an obvious misogynist, capable of alarming and hateful bouts of anger and cruelty toward friends, children, and colleagues."

This sort of wit, left unchecked, quickly metastasizes into something else: Snark. It's not about spontaneous creativity; it's about speedy meanness. Wit means assembling disparate ideas to delight; snark is just rehashing the same contempt in new ways. Still, the border between the two is at times blurry. In *The Snark Handbook: A Reference Guide for Verbal Sparring,* Lawrence Dorfman defines his subject first as "biting wit," then as a "smartass remark" or "slyly disparaging comment." But compare that to David Denby's polemic *Snark,* defined on its jacket as "a witless and charmless way of speaking." It's fitting that these contradictory definitions are for a word made up in 1874 by Lewis Carroll, the master of literary nonsense. In *The Hunting of the Snark: An Agony in Eight Fits,* in which nine men and one beaver set sail with a blank map to hunt an animal that may or may not exist. It is a nonsense poem, perhaps the all-time best, and it's not at all snarky in the present meaning of the word. (Some also claim that snark is an elision of "snide remark," an etymology that probably makes too much sense to be true.) Carroll's hunters never really say why they've taken on this mission—it's a "glorious duty," we're told—and Carroll said the rare beast was impossible to explain. (Obviously he was right.) First, it tastes "meagre and hollow, but crisp." Then there's its "slowness at taking a jest"— when it encounters actual wit, "It will sigh like a thing that is deeply depressed." And then there are some that "have feathers, and bite," which aren't to be confused with those that "have whiskers, and scratch."

Clearly, the hunters of the snark should have abandoned their random island and focused their hunt on the comment boards of the modern internet. There, snark prevails. The first snide remark on a news story is a sad little badge of honor for these beasts, whether it's attacking the figures in the story or falling back on that time-tested chestnut, "HOW IS THIS NEWS?!!?" No new light will be shed in all this heat: They're there to simulate outrage, ennui, disgust or something equally, predictably negative. It might as well be a script, and it's not a particularly original one.

From those comment boards—the footprints of the beast— the hunters would almost certainly track snark in the internet age to its presumed source, the New York website Gawker, on which it has been living and breeding since 2003. But the border between wit and snark can be hard to define, and Gawker has more often than not straddled it.

And then in late 2013, Gawker writer Tom Scocca complicated things even further with "On Smarm," a fairly brilliant essay explaining that everyone was going after the wrong five-letter S-word. The key passage:

> Snark is often conflated with cynicism, which is a troublesome mis-reading. Snark may speak in cynical terms about a cynical world, but it is not cynicism itself. It is a theory of cynicism.
>
> The practice of cynicism is smarm.

Scocca defines smarm as "an assumption of the forms of seriousness, of virtue, of constructiveness, without the substance," a way to fill the empty hole where your moral fiber is supposed to reside with umbrage. It is likely at the heart of most anti-Gawker tirades, and it is most definitely the enemy of wit. If you must pick a poison, go with snark over smarm.

For our purposes, though, let's call snark good sense that scorches, as compared with our definition of wit as good sense that sparkles. Snark may be necessary and defensible, but it's not the subject of this book.

We are much more interested in the kind, good-hearted people who use wit to spread warmth. To be spontaneous and to be creative are generally seen as positive attributes, so to be both—to be witty—should at least be the sum of its parts. In the words of Joseph Addison, wit is a resemblance of ideas "that gives delight and surprise." To offer this to a listener is a gift, and there's nothing cruel about that. These people don't have to be saints; they just have to use their linguistic gifts to make the world ever so slightly better. Their effect is not to use their skill to attack one person but rather to lift many with the unparalleled joy that comes from watching an agile mind at play. Compassionate wit is admittedly not as common as cruel wit, though it certainly ought to be.

A Starting Point for Compassionate Wit

Aristotle called "ready wit" one of the virtues of human interaction. He did so in the same book that described the Golden Mean, the idea that perfection in all things is to be found between the extremes. Wit, as he describes it, lies between the buffoon, who will try to make light of everything, and the boor, who is in the dark about it all. The buffoon "is the slave of his sense of humor, and spares neither himself nor others if he can raise a laugh, and says things none of which a man of refinement would say, and to some of which he would not even listen." Contrast that to the boor, who "is useless for such social intercourse; for he contributes nothing and finds fault with everything."

(It is in this same book that Oscar Wilde found early support for the way he lived his life, making the following note in the margins: "Man makes his end for himself out of himself: no end is imposed by external considerations, he must realize his true nature, must be what nature orders, so must discover what his nature is.")

Obviously there is some overlap with the general idea of humor here, but much of what he says applies to wit. Too much distributed too carelessly will inevitably be cruel, and that's when you end up saying things unworthy of a man of refinement. More surprising is the other end of the spectrum, the idea that when you entirely keep wit out of your conversation, you end up an unenlightened boor. In moderation, wit will make you good company; without it, you're going to bore those around you senseless.

This definition lines up nicely with the fact ancient Greeks would refer to wit as salt. Attic salt, meaning from the Athenians, to this day means a refined sort of wit. Without it, food is bland and quickly goes bad. With the right amount, meals are much more delicious. Too much, though, and the food is once again inedible.

To ask if salt is cruel or compassionate

This guy is pompous.

would be like asking if it is happy or sad. Salt in your wounds is certainly a cruel application, but a bit of salt on your chocolate bar is an artisanal treat. With wit, as with salt, it's more interesting to focus on the great things it can do.

The Bad Rap

Groucho Marx was a classic example of the unfortunate and unfair reputation wits get for being cruel. This sentiment is threaded through his obituaries.

"Because of his acid tongue, Groucho gave the impression of being a misanthrope," read the report by the Associated Press in 1977. "He wasn't. He felt very strongly about causes and lent his support to Presidents Roosevelt, Truman and Kennedy."

That weak defense is further eroded by lines like "His constant irreverence mitigated against friend-making. More than most comedians, Groucho was a loner." and "longtime friends like Jack Benny and George Burns could not feel comfortable with Groucho because his wit could strike in any direction."

Marx may well have been an unhappy man—his personal letters reveal a constant fear of failure and each of his three marriages ended in painful divorce—but it's too convenient to equate his unhappiness with his wit. Plenty of people are dissatisfied with life; only a few have the facility to creatively demonstrate this dissatisfaction.

"Occasionally you hear admirers of his wit opine that he was probably a cold man, perhaps because wit by itself can be a chilling thing," writes Dick Cavett in his introduction to a collection of Groucho Marx's letters to his daughter—letters that, it should be noted, are consistent and loving if occasionally impatient. "It seemed clear to me [as a teenager watching *You Bet Your Life*] that he was always good-natured and that only those insulated against humor and devoid of perception could take umbrage."

And indeed, the *New York Times* obituary made a similar distinction. "[G]roucho's expertly delivered, rapid-fire insults were more mad than maddening; they weren't really unkind, for they evolved from his interest in humor that deflated rather than annihilated," wrote Albin Krebs, who then quotes a 1968 interview in which Marx claims that his humor "made people laugh at themselves, rather than the sort that prevails today—the sick, black, merely smart-aleck stuff designed to provoke malicious laughter at the other fellow."

There is clearly a distinction here, and only those who refuse to see it will contend that all wit is cruel. But it's worth looking to a couple of wits who managed to practice their art without forcing their obituarists to prove that they were, in fact, good people. Admittedly, that's a pretty low bar, but think of it this way: There's nowhere to go but up.

The Kindest Wit

Robert Benchley, a charter member of the Algonquin Round Table, once summed up his life by saying he was born on the Isle of Wight in 1807, arrested for bigamy and murder in Port Said in 1817, married Princess Anastasia of Portugal in 1831, wrote

Uncle Tom's Cabin in 1850, started *Les Misérables* in 1870 but let Victor Hugo finish it and, upon his death in 1871, was buried in Westminster Abbey.

The facts are slightly less remarkable but still worthy of note: Drama critic for *Vanity Fair* and the *New Yorker*, winner of an Academy Award for a short film about sleep, teetotaler turned alcoholic, prolific layabout, warmhearted man and one of the Great Wits. The combination of these final two attributes made him universally loved, a man who enthusiastically enlisted everyone he met in his campaign against life's indignities.

His best witticisms drag the absurd into the everyday, generally leaving everyone better for having heard them. He famously mocked any attempts to explain how humor worked—"tests made on five hundred subjects in the Harvard School of Applied Laughter, using the Mergenthaler Laugh Detector, have shown that, unless a joke begins with the letter 'W,' the laughter is forced, almost unpleasant at times"—and as his son Nathaniel put it, his humor was "sometimes mad, sometimes penetrating, and sometimes based on nothing more than word associations."

Even when he was playing offense, it was hard to take offense. When Benchley asked a uniformed man in front of a restaurant to hail him a cab and was coolly informed that his supposed doorman was in fact an admiral in the U.S. Navy, he quickly changed his request to a battleship.

There is something very warm about Benchley, both in his film appearances and his writing. His wit is omnipresent but never threatening. His close friend Dorothy Parker often expressed her dissatisfaction with herself, her work and her world through her facility with language, and many of her earliest jibes—"This is not a book to be tossed aside gently. It should be thrown with great force."—came in her reviews. This might seem a necessary part of the critic's job, but Benchley managed to both avoid making his name synonymous with putdowns and prevent that sort of acidic thinking from seeping into his character. His reviews matched Parker's in clever barbs—"It was one of those plays in which all the actors unfortunately enunciated very clearly," for instance—but they didn't stick to him. Some might note that reputation management was and probably still is much easier for a WASPy Harvard man than a Jewish woman. On balance, though, the difference is that while both critics could wield a knife, Benchley would rarely twist it.

Making Light of Verse

Even if you don't think you know Ogden Nash, you most probably do. If you know that "Candy is dandy / But liquor is quicker," then you have memorized his poem "Reflections on Ice-Breaking." The man behind that rhyme, its 1960s addendum ("Pot is not") and several thousand more like it managed a remarkable feat of simultaneously being a well-respected modern poet and a beloved popular phrase-turner. Who else fits that description?

As the poet Dana Gioia asks in his introduction to a Nash biography, "What other American poet of the Modernist era published best-selling collections of verse, collaborated in Hollywood screenplays, authored Broadway lyrics, recited his work on radio variety shows, and served as a television game show panelist—

all the while writing poems on contract for several of America's
biggest magazines?"

Nash wrote what is technically called "light verse," a term
that essentially defines the rest of the poetry world as heavy verse.
And though that's not what it's supposed to mean, maybe it's
true. (It's reminiscent of a similar Dave Barry bit about popular music; if you're listening to jazz, classical or world, you're listening to unpopular music.) Nash did hit on big themes in his
poetry—mortality, the impermanence of love, civilization and its
discontents—but he often did so while rhyming words and near-
words like "insouciance" and "nouciance," "snuffly" and "luffly,"
"Canada" and "veranda," and "panther" and "anther." He could
do serious or silly, in both tone and content, and neither was taken
as a betrayal of the other.

In a sense, his light verse was all about making light of verse.
Anyone who has perused the greeting-card aisle of the drugstore
will recognize the age-old challenge Nash is implicitly mocking:
Poems are more memorable if they rhyme, but they're completely

ruined if they sound forced. Think of every song that tries to find a rhyme for "love," and then discount the ones that cheat with the word "of." P. G. Wodehouse put it best in his essay "On the Writing of Lyrics," published in *Vanity Fair* way back in 1917:

> *No lyricist wants to keep linking "love" with "skies above" and "turtle dove," but what can he do? You can't do a thing with "shove"; and "glove" is just one of those aloof words which are not good mixers. And—mark the brutality of the thing—there is no word you can substitute for "love." It is just as if they did it on purpose.*

Ogden Nash avoids such flowery rhymes in favor of silly ones. Instead of obvious ones that work, he opts for unlikely ones that don't quite work—and thus, in a wonderful way, work better than you'd expect. The Italian term for it is "*sprezzatura*," and though this generally describes a studied nonchalance in dress or wardrobe—the way a Roman gentleman will be featured on street-style blogs in a houndstooth sports jacket and tennis shorts, for instance—it fits this poetry quite well. Something about knowing that he knows better makes it all hold together. "Who wants my jellyfish? I'm not sellyfish!" isn't so much a play on words as a linguistic pratfall. It's not so bad it's good, but rather so good at being bad that it's good.

Does this qualify as compassion? Think of it this way: If cruel wit is employed to obliterate a single target, compassionate wit is more likely to invigorate a large audience. If Nash's rhymes, be they read in the *New Yorker* or heard on the radio, brought a smile to an otherwise gray day, then they have succeeded.

(A cruel wit might argue that poems like "The Jellyfish" actually cause the listener to suffer. Said wit should try reciting that poem next time she's in conversation with a five-year-old.)

A nice evocation of the effect Nash's work had on the world comes again from Dana Gioia, who writes about how his mother, a working-class Mexican-American woman who worked nights at the phone company and did not subscribe to the *New Yorker*, could recite a number of his poems by heart. "God in his wisdom made the fly / And then forgot to tell us why," he reports her saying every time she had to swat one. For all parties on this end of the flyswatter, that qualifies as compassionate wit.

{ QUIP QUIZ }

1. "I only believe in the SEBF Association: Everyone But Fields." —**W. C. Fields**

2. "To be _____ requires a certain thoughtlessness; to be cruel, the opposite." —**George Murray**

3. "When I was young I looked like Al _____, but I lacked his compassion." —**Oscar Levant**

4. "My heart goes out to him. Sort of. Because _____ depends on how you spent your day." —**George Saunders**

5. "All cruel people describe themselves as paragons of _____." —**Tennessee Williams**

Screw	Mean	Capone	Empathy	Frankness

Compassion
Wit List

- [ ] Have more grace than Ricky Gervais
- [ ] Be a dash like Ogden Nash
- [ ] Don't be cruel to a heart that's true

ELEVEN

Conversation

Featuring: THE FRENCH CLOWN'S GOLDEN RULE, MAURICE
BARRYMORE, THE DEMISE OF THE ALGONQUIN ROUND TABLE
AND THE GENIUS OF TOM STOPPARD'S TOFFEE APPLES

◆ ◆ ◆

To be witty in conversation is a bad idea. Yes, this is a book
about wit, and yes, conversation is an element of spontaneous creativity, but to fill your conversations with spontaneous
creativity is a recipe for disaster.

The Great Wits were all great talkers. This doesn't mean they
were great conversationalists. It's one thing to speak well; quite
another to listen well; and a third altogether to combine the two
into great conversation. As the British writer William Hazlitt
noted, "A perpetual succession of good things puts an end to
common conversation." Wit alone won't cut it.

Realizing that it's not what you talk about but how you talk
about it—and how little you talk about it—is the first step. From
there, it's all about everything we've covered up to here: The bit
of knowledge supplied by hustle, the flow, the intuition, the con-

fidence, the refreshment, and in smaller measures the righteousness, charm, perhaps the romance, always the resilience, and
underlying it all—perhaps most important of all—the compassion.

At its heart, a conversation is about listening, not talking. To
be thought of as a good conversationalist means you are judged
as such by the person to whom you are speaking. When you
put it in those terms—realizing the judge is not some Athenian
guardian of high wit but the guy standing in front of you—the
course of action becomes clear. Make this guy feel good and
you've succeeded.

Rebecca Northan is a woman who has made a career out of
successful conversation. She boils it all down to the Golden
Rule. You want to be listened to, to be encouraged, to be engaged
and, above all, to be loved—and that's how you should do unto
others.

Northan has done so around the world in the guise of Mimi,
a French clown. (The costume consists only of the nose; otherwise Northan's attire is chic Parisian black.) She is the co-star of
a one-woman show called *Blind Date*, the star being the lucky

gentleman plucked from the audience to go on a first date with Mimi. This may sound like cringe-worthy improv, but in practice it's neither of those things. She calls it "spontaneous theater," and it generally leaves all parties with a warm glow of appreciation.

"What we're working toward—unlike when you go to a comedy club and see improv where they drag someone up on stage for five minutes and the comedy is at that person's expense—what we're doing is conspiring to make you look good for the entire time you're with us, and to treat you like a guest and make sure you're having a nice time," Northan explains.

She's convinced all her dates are lovable and she has a whole toolbox of tricks to make sure they come off that way. First, she treats the person she's speaking with as though he's a guest in her home: "You wouldn't have someone over to your house and the first thing they ask about, you say, *no!* That makes them look bad and it also makes them feel really bad."

Kindness is her MO and she reports that it rarely if ever fails. Admittedly, she screens her volunteers in the lobby before the show, making sure to eliminate the people who are way too eager to be on stage ("It's not normal as a primate to want to be looked at. Those of us who are actors, who can even find a way to be comfortable on stage: That's not normal.") and the clearly nerve-racked, people dragged to the show against their will or judgment. Still, some of her subjects will turn nasty on stage, behavior Northan credits entirely to nerves. "But because I love that person for saying yes in the first place, I recognize that they're having a defensive reaction and I work to calm them down."

Her next tactic is simple: Open-ended questions. "And *real* open-ended questions. One thing I've found is that to truly ask an open-ended question is really to let go of control. You really put the steering wheel or the conch or whatever image you want to use into the person's hands, because you have no idea how they're going to answer the question." This creates spontaneity, meaning all you need to do is add creativity. But it's much harder than it sounds because we bring bundles of assumptions into every conversation, thinking we know the other person's deal long before we've given him or her a chance to say anything. Without realizing it, we use conversations as a chance to prove our assumptions, and we do that with closed yes-or-no questions. It's both inherently logical and a total buzzkill.

Without realizing it, we use conversations as a chance to prove our assumptions.

All of which is noble and good, but by this point you might humbly note that you're ready to be witty: Can you do so without grabbing the conversational steering wheel and causing a social traffic accident?

Yes, Northan says, but with care. In her show there's plenty of room for her stories, but they are carefully deployed in the service of helping the other person. She'll ask an open question, for instance, and then there might be some hesitation. She'll let her date think for a bit, but then, "in order to make them look good and not like you've stumped them, you go, well, for example, here's a story from my life. Me sharing my story will allow

you to relax. It'll also jog your memory. Or if they do have a story, I might say, *Oh yeah, I totally know how you feel, here's a time I felt the same.* Either I lead by example or I reciprocate so that the person doesn't feel alone."

Again, it's conversation as compassion: An unorthodox way to approach your next cocktail party, but one that's been proven effective both in theory and in practice.

All Talk

Now that we've made the most important part of conversation clear, we can move on to the talky bits. To be described as "all talk," is, no matter how you spin it, an insult. Some wits have embraced it, and though they are often remembered via lament— if only he would have just shut up and written something!—they are at least remembered.

When Oscar Wilde was just finding his footing in London society, he arranged to be introduced to a famed Polish actress by the name of Helena Modjeska. "What has he done, this young man, that one meets him everywhere?" the actress wondered, according to Richard Ellmann's biography. "Oh yes he talks well, but what has he done?" (Wilde's response, that "talk itself is a sort of spiritualized action," was one of his weaker ripostes, and he obviously went on to prove that he could do plenty.)

Modjeska on occasion played opposite Maurice Barrymore, one of the great all-talkers in history, the owner of a mind that, in the memorable words of one report, "glittered in clubdom."

A famous exchange between the two had Barrymore forgetting his lines and embarrassing her on stage, then attempting to further embarrass her. As reported in the syndicated "Wisecracks of the Famous" column decades after his death, Modjeska said, "Ah, what an ingrate you are! To treat me like this after I made your reputation for you in America!" To which Barrymore responds, "I will admit that my acting tonight was not all it should have been. But let me remind you, madam, that I was a well-known actor in America when most people thought Modjeska was a mouth wash or a headache cure."

As the *New York Times* stated in his obituary in 1901, Barrymore "was seen to his best advantage in a circle of friends. His splendid qualities as a raconteur, his flashing wit, and his readiness at repartee made him the life of many a party." A Cambridge-educated Englishman, he found fame in the United States (and once, upon being told by a British producer that his "beastly American accent" was unsuitable for the London stage, he replied, "That's odd, they tell me on the other side that I won't do on account of my beastly English accent. What on earth am I to do—give recitations on the transatlantic steamers?")

The patriarch of the famous Barrymore acting dynasty, though well accomplished on the stage, would spend his leisure time carousing with his fellow actors, regaling them with stories of the plays he would one day write. Partly in jest, his fellow actor Wilton Lackaye wrote his epitaph during one of their late-night parties:

> HE TALKED BENEATH THE MOON
> AND HE SLEPT BENEATH THE SUN;
> HE LED THE LIFE OF GOING TO DO
> AND DIED WITH NOTHING DONE.

This comes from an obituary of Barrymore, whose decline was perhaps the most horrible an actor could imagine: On stage, he forgot his lines and started ranting, and was committed to an asylum shortly thereafter.

Barrymore did command the stage, start a dynasty and become a legend of the theater, so it's a touch harsh to declare his life a complete failure. But then, his talk was the yardstick by which his accomplishments were measured. Wilde did talk a good game in his early twenties, but then he lived up to it. Bragging about achievements he had yet to realize was in keeping with Wilde's confidence, but it's not an advisable course of action for mere mortals, particularly those who like to spend their spare time partying.

The Algonquin Round Table

When it comes to the history of furniture, there are really only two round tables of note: King Arthur's and Dorothy Parker's. Sadly, both are more or less fictions. Arthur's was a symbol of his wisdom; to keep his knights from feuding, he made sure all the seats were equal. If that sort of pettiness seems below a knight, keep in mind this was the fifth century and likely a myth. Parker's was a symbol of her wit; a magical lunch date at which the cleverest people in a clever town convened to crack wise.

But did they actually converse? For a brief, shining moment, yes.

The whole affair began in 1919 as a practical joke that backfired. Alexander Woollcott, the dean of New York's theater critics, was known to be a pompous and self-important type who never tired of speaking about what a great war he had. Two irritated publicists wanted a bit of light-hearted revenge and they came up with an elaborate scheme to get it. They invited Woollcott and all his peers to the Algonquin Hotel to formally welcome him back from the First World War. The publicists arranged to have their target's name misspelled on banners and in the program, which consisted entirely of speeches by Woollcott. They had hoped this series of subtle digs would add up to just the right amount of humiliation, but they got the math wrong. It's unclear whether Woollcott got the joke and then got the better of it by playing along, or simply missed the cues and reveled in the attention. Either way, everyone had fun, no one got the prank, they decided to make it a regular thing, and thus the Algonquin Round Table was born.

The fact that all the members were journalists or publicists is no accident: Their mentions of their lunchtime activities flowed directly into print, making the event famous before the year was out. Everyone was well served—the journalists got free food, the publicists had daily one-stop access to every big byline in town, the hotel became a destination—even when they may have been overserved (this was Prohibition, though, so the bathtub gin would only have come out off premises; the lunches weren't accompanied by anything stronger than tea).

In the early days, the conversation was said to be lively, respectful and, above all, actual conversation: A give-and-take of anecdotes, witticisms, information and opinion to listeners hungry for all of the above. These critics were, after all, lower in the food chain than Woollcott and benefited from bringing him the best morsels of gossip. In the words of Dorothy Parker's biographer Marion Meade: "She was truly at her best in conversation, where she presented the routine she had perfected: demure, deadpan expression, the disparity between a patrician voice modulated to just above a whisper and her inexhaustible repertoire of obscenities."

Soon, though, the order of things fell into place. The charter members had their conversations, but the up-and-comers would bring their best lines preformed and ready to go. The meat-to-salt ratio was slowly thrown out of whack, and soon there was nothing but wisecracks. Eventually, as the Algonquin's reputation outgrew its reality, even the likes of Parker and Benchley were preparing bits for public consumption.

That's not how conversation works. As Parker said bitterly (an adverb that could be applied to the vast majority of her later quips), by 1923 or so the Round Table was just a bunch of wannabes who "came there to be heard by one another. 'Did you hear what I said last night?'" But asking if anyone heard your witticism is the surest sign that you're doing it wrong.

And enough Tablers have reported the same sad fact. Heywood Hale Broun, son of Round Table regular Heywood Broun, wrote in 1968 of his father that he "even rehearsed his humor, and would sometimes take me along to lunch so that I could pipe out straight lines for laborious puns which I now remember with affection but not enough admiration to repeat."

Enough said, in more ways than one. The legend was set, and the fact that so many tried to keep it going after it was clearly over only made it more of a legend.

Dialogue and Tom Stoppard

The difference between one person talking aloud to himself or herself and two people in conversation seems like the difference between crazy and sane. That may be true but it's not binary: Just as there's plenty of interesting gray between the extremes of perfectly, boringly sane and plumb loco—though the psychiatric establishment likely won't confirm this statement, that's where you'll find all the most interesting people—there is something to be said (aloud) for talking to yourself. As Guildenstern points out in Tom Stoppard's *Rosencrantz and Guildenstern Are Dead*, "a man talking sense to himself is no madder than a man talking nonsense not to himself."

The subject here isn't the guy muttering to himself on the bus or the woman cursing aloud on the park bench—though these days, those characters may simply be talking into a wireless phone headset, meaning their problem is more with their manners than their minds. It's about playing out a dialogue in your head (or aloud), like a chess master figuring out where the board might be headed. You might try to play this sort of game in everyday conversation, but it's of limited appeal and once again may only serve to oversalt the meal. As we learned from those in the flow, you have to be present to be fully engaged.

Jonathan Swift ably mocked those who would studiously prepare for casual discussions in his book *Polite Conversation*, billed as an "infallible remedy" when you run out of things to talk about. The back-and-forth of these types was a series of clichés, maxims and potted replies, the sort of thing we could easily replicate these days by having the voice controls of two smartphones engage in pleasantries that sound like intelligent discussion but are actually a series of algorithm-generated sound bites.

COLONEL: This wine should be eaten, it is too good to be
  drunk.

LORD SMART: I'm very glad you like it; and pray don't
  spare it.

COLONEL: No my lord; I'll never starve in a cook's shop.

But if you play out a conversation not as some sort of
Machiavellian practice but purely to amuse yourself, well, then
you've stumbled back into our definition of wit. Take this extract
from an interview Stoppard, the great British playwright, did
with Jon Bradshaw for *New York* magazine in 1977:

STOPPARD: The plays tend to give an impression of
  effervescence and style and wit for their own sake and
  thereby obscure what to me is the core of the toffee
  apple.

BRADSHAW: The toffee apple?

STOPPARD: A toffee apple, American readers, is a sort of
  hot dog, taken from Sanskrit. . . . *Tof* meaning hot and
  Ap, a sort of dog.

BRADSHAW: Are you prepared to stand by that?

STOPPARD: Well, I write fiction because it's a way of
  making statements I can disown. And I write plays
  because dialogue is the most respectable way of
  contradicting myself.

BRADSHAW: Not bad. May I quote you on that?

STOPPARD: There's no point in being quoted if one isn't
  going to be quotable.

Admittedly this sounds like a softball interview, and so it seemed like a natural progression when in 2005, the Royal Society for Literature invited Stoppard to just cut out the middleman and interview himself. His first question was "Why are you interviewing yourself?" to which he answered, "Because I don't like being interviewed by other people." (And way back in 1967, when he was first told of a glowing *New York Times* review for *Rosencrantz*, he is said to have turned to his wife and said, "Question: Mr. Stoppard, what is your play about? Answer: It's about to make me rich.")

In both cases you could say he prefers softball questions, or, since he's British, whatever the cricket version of a softball is, which brings us to the famous cricket bat speech from Stoppard's *The Real Thing*:

This thing here, which looks like a wooden club, is actually several pieces of particular wood cunningly put together in a certain way so that the whole thing is sprung, like a dance floor. It's for hitting cricket balls with. If you get it right, the cricket ball will travel two hundred yards in four seconds, and all you've done is give it a knock like knocking the top off a bottle of stout, and it makes a noise like a trout taking a fly. What we're trying to do is to write cricket bats, so that when we throw up an idea and give it a little knock, it might . . . travel.

And there you have his perfect explanation for what binds style and substance in his plays, and the ideas that are the core of the hot dog. His work fits in a great tradition of Socratic dialogue, of teasing ideas out by having two characters discuss them rather than one know-it-all narrator tell you what's what. It also lets him set up brilliant jokes, exchanges, puns and epigrams, which is a nice side effect. Among the asides in an argument about what to put on the record player in *The Real Thing*, for instance, is the observation, with reference to Buddy Holly's premature death, that "[I]f Beethoven had been killed in a plane crash at twenty-two, the history of music would have been very different. As would the history of aviation, of course."

In interviews, Stoppard displays the magpie mind he described in chapter one, and there seems to be little difference between him talking to a reporter and his characters talking in plays. An interview, however, is not a conversation. In the former, one person is asking questions and acting as a proxy for an audience; No one cares what the interviewer thinks unless it directly pertains to what the interviewee just said. A conversation is more like verbal tennis—one person serves and the other returns, but the roles change fluidly and quickly throughout the game. And—wouldn't you know it—verbal tennis was invented, or at least introduced to the canon, by one Tom Stoppard in *Rosencrantz and Guildenstern Are Dead*. In the play it was simply called the game of questions but scored like tennis, but the 1990 film puts Tim Roth and Gary Oldman on a tennis court as they play.

All of this doesn't prove Stoppard, as a Great Wit, is great at actual conversations, but something rarer: He creates perfect conversations on his own, and they are found in his work like diamonds in a crown. And when you watch his work, either on stage or screen, you'll inadvertently already be halfway toward a great conversation: You'll be listening. That, in a roundabout way, is the final and best lesson on wit and the art of discourse: Practiced lines and hardened opinions kill conversation just as surely as listening nurtures it. If it's to be an aimless, intellectual adventure—as it must be—lose the roadmap and follow the road.

And so we return to Rebecca Northan, who deserves to be listened to precisely because she is a professional listener. The subtitle of this book describes wit as the art of being interesting, but conversation is as much about the art of being interested. In Northan's experience, that shouldn't be difficult to do provided you ask the right questions.

"I have never had a human being sit opposite me who is boring," she said. "How you choose to live your life is not the way I choose to live my life, and why you made those different decisions is interesting. Every life is interesting."

{ QUIP QUIZ }

1. "There's no such thing as conversation. It is an illusion. There are interesting _____, that is all."

   —Rebecca West

2. "The wit of conversation consists more in finding it in _____ than in showing a great deal yourself: he who goes from your conversation pleased with himself and his own wit is perfectly pleased with you."

   —Jean de La Bruyère

3. "She plunged into a sea of platitudes, and with the powerful breaststroke of a channel swimmer made her confident way towards the white cliffs of the _____."

—W. Somerset Maugham

4. "Let us make a special effort to stop _____ with each other, so we can have some conversation."

—Mark Twain

5. "Conversation should be like _____; up go the balls and plates, up and over, in and out, good solid objects that glitter in the footlights and fall with a bang if you miss them."

—Evelyn Waugh

Monologues	Others	Obvious	Communicating	Juggling

CONVERSATION
wit list
_____

☐ Reciprocate, mate!
☐ Keep the rally going
☐ If you fail to plan,
   you plan to flow
☐ Everyone's interesting?

TWELVE

Brevity

Featuring: THAT LINE ABOUT BREVITY THAT WE
MUST REFERENCE, "THE ARISTOCRATS," RICKY GERVAIS,
DISHWASHER TETRIS, SEINFELD TODAY VS. SEINFELD CURRENT
DAY, PATTON OSWALT AND BRAWNY PAPER TOWELS

◆ ◆ ◆

The relationship between brevity and wit was made clear in *Hamlet*, thus allowing us to wrap this chapter up in just under 140 characters.

But wait! Just as the scheming Polonius reminded us of wit's soul in the middle of a long and nonsensical speech, the joys of brevity are perhaps best discussed at length. Consider Strunk and White's famous entry under the heading "Omit Needless Words":

> *Vigorous writing is concise. A sentence should contain no unnecessary words, a paragraph no unnecessary sentences. . . . This requires not that the writer make all his sentences short, or that he avoid all detail and treat his subjects only in outline, but that every word tell.*

In speech, the idea of making every word tell is much looser than in print. Many stories owe much of their dramatic effect to the windup, and there are plenty of jokes that require a lengthy setup to maximize the payoff. Take, for example, the infamous joke "The Aristocrats," the subject of comedic legend and a 2005 documentary. In short, it involves a family visiting a talent agent and describing their act. In long, the descriptions of the act violate every social norm the comedian can work in, and legend has it that really advanced versions take up to an hour to tell. In closing, the gobsmacked talent agent asks, *"What do you call it?"* And the father replies, *"The Aristocrats."* If it seems unfunny, that's because it is. The middle bit, and just how inventively obscene it can get, is the part that makes it work, to the extent that it works on anyone other than professional comedians who prize its obtuseness. But even they would never commit it to the page, and not because they fear the wrath of Strunk and White. Cocktail party conversation and technical writing are very different things, unless we're discussing a technical manual on cocktail parties, the results of which likely wouldn't produce a very memorable evening.

That said, wit is more often than not punchy and to the point. One needs to be fast, and a sure way to get your words out quickly is to ensure there aren't too many of them. Which brings us, quickly, to the online microblogging service we all know as Twitter.

Twitter and Its Malcontents

There should be no doubt the Great Wits, all of whom aimed at the largest possible audience, would be on Twitter. "It is foolish to talk to a few hundred when you can talk to millions," George Bernard Shaw told an interviewer on his 1933 trip to the U.S. He was talking about the advantages of radio over regular old oratory but this certainly applies to social media.

As Jonah Peretti, the creator of BuzzFeed, tweeted on March 2, 2010, "Twitter is a simple service used by smart people. Facebook is a smart service used by simple people." Smart people have indeed made the most of Twitter, turning it into a vital medium for news, opinion and 140-character reports on what they ate for lunch. But a sizable contingent of smart people have also made the least of it, declaring it a symptom of all that is wrong with the modern world. Certainly those who decry the coarsening of the culture brought about by Twitter don't spare the verbiage, though they often should. Their arguments, as quickly delivered by a straw man: It's trite, it's overwhelming, it's ephemeral and it's making us stupid. But just as everyone who uses their voice isn't necessarily worth listening to, everyone who tweets needn't be followed. If it's too much to follow, you're following too many people. Life is ephemeral; ask any Buddhist. And while the act of refreshing the Twitter app on the iPhone is disconcertingly like something a laboratory animal would do for the next hit of dopamine, it doesn't mean we're stupid. Rather, a technology that taps into our addiction to information has been placed in our hands, and of course we're going to use and occasionally abuse it.

It's important to distinguish what Twitter is from what we might like it to be. In theory, Twitter is perfect for aphorisms. In practice, not so much. The perfect aphorism is a distillation of knowledge, a boiling down of life experience to the facts of one perfect sentence. Twitter isn't so much what's boiled down as the steam that rises off. While an aphorism is probably less than 140 characters and ideally shared with as many people as possible, it's also designed to last. It is not supposed to be ephemeral. So the fact that Twitter isn't full of useful original maxims just shows that it's working. Were we to design a similar service to capture hard-earned truths, we might force people to pay per character and then have their words chiseled into fine Italian marble. (This business idea is free for anyone who wants it.)

At its best, Twitter can transform the world to an immediate and egalitarian conversation, where we may differ in our number of followers but we all have the same character limit. And as such, it's a grand arena where wit stands a fighting chance against the armies of dullness.

Take, for instance, a 2013 tweet by television host and self-proclaimed "hardcore huntress" Melissa Bachman that accompanied a photo of her beaming over the corpse of a jungle cat: "An incredible day hunting in South Africa. Stalked inside 60-yards on this beautiful male lion—what a hunt!" There was plenty of outrage and vitriol, though it wasn't immediate. Ten days after that initial tweet made the rounds, Bachman disappeared from social media. Fourteen days later, Ricky Gervais responded by quoting the tweet verbatim and appending the words "spot the typo." Subtly crass and perfectly devastating, this is a modern version of the cutting comebacks of Churchill and Wilde—and there's no need to say you had to be there, because for the price of an internet connection, you could be. (Note also the timing of this retort; for all the immediacy of modern communication, a fortnight passed in between comment and insult. It wasn't spontaneous, though it felt that way.)

But with more than half a billion users around the world, concentrating only on the ripostes of comedy gods is like picking out the prettiest grains of sand on the beach. To get a larger view of what Twitter wit was, is and will be, we should start with the first-ever book on the matter.

Brevity's Rainbow

Twitter was founded in 2006. Three years later the book *Twitter Wit* was published. Billed as "An Authorized Collection of the Funniest Tweets of All Time"—a use of "All Time" that makes VH1 countdowns of the all-time best music videos look worthy of the Smithsonian (spoiler alert: the years 50,000 BC to 1975 will be woefully underrepresented in the top ten)—the paperback now reads like a chronicle of a simpler era. Back then, a site called Favrd collected the best tweets and Ashton Kutcher was the biggest name you could follow. But even at three, the basic strains of Twitter wit were coming into focus. A careful study of this book reveals that there are:

1. **Late-night monologue jokes**, the sort of mildly amusing and topical one-liners designed for delivery by an aging white man standing in front of a curtain. For example:

   @bonerparty: When Morgan Freeman reads a book, whose voice is in his head?

   @earlkabong: So now Blagojevich has been double-impeached, which sounds like a Ben & Jerry's flavor.

   @danielleu: Leno criticized Twitter for having a permanent record of anything you've ever said. Sounds almost as horrible as taping yourself everyday.

2. **Steven Wright–Mitch Hedberg observations**, the sort
   of lines that have so permeated the culture, you picture a
   guy deadpanning into a microphone as you read them.
   Such as:

   @swamibooba: If plungers could talk, you wouldn't
   own one.

   @johntunger: PSA: 'Instant coffee' isn't either.

   @secretsquirrel: I've yet to see a pair of boots that
   weren't made for walking.

3. **Real-time asides**, a category that gets points for originality: You can't imagine anyone speaking these aloud, so it's
   safe to say they wouldn't exist without Twitter.

   @adrianchen: Eating an entire frittata. Note: Devise
   method for making half a frittata.

   @robot_operator: Well the good news is that now I
   know what poison ivy looks like.

   @d_g: I just got a new high score at Dishwasher Tetris!

(These are also the most artificial of tweets, in that they describe the person doing an everyday activity at that exact moment, when, in actual fact, the person briefly stopped engaging
in that activity, pulled out an internet-connected device and pro-
ceeded to compose a pithy message nonchalantly describing said
activity. If you saw that person, he or she would be hunched over

a smartphone. Once you start picturing this, it really deflates the cinema verité effect.)

In 2010, no less an authority than Stephen Fry selected the "most beautiful tweet ever tweeted." (Again, the disclaimer on the word "ever" applies.) The winner, Marc MacKenzie, a medical physicist from Edmonton, Canada, took home the title with a tweet that firmly fits into Type 2 Twitter Wit:

> I believe we can build a better world! Of course, it'll take a whole lot of rock, water & dirt. Also, not sure where to put it.

It is, it must be acknowledged, a pretty good tweet. There is the banal expression, followed by an unexpected and thus funny practical extension, and brought home by a further elaboration of this thought. As MacKenzie told the BBC after winning the award, "A certain percentage of tweets are tired cliché phrases, so when they come into my head I think, *That won't do.* I can't stand triteness, so I always look for the ridiculousness in trite."

In a way, this is the hallmark of some of the best aphorists. "The best things in life are free," is much better rendered as "The best things in life aren't things," for example. And we need only turn to Oscar Wilde to see a life's worth of common phrases made both more clever and more true—wittier, in a word—by his turning them inside out.

To wit, from *The Picture of Dorian Gray*: "I hate vulgar realism in literature. The man who could call a spade a spade should be compelled to use one. It is the only thing he is fit for." Or from a letter in 1890: "People who count their chickens before they are hatched, act very wisely, because chickens run about so absurdly that it is impossible to count them accurately."

Unfortunately, the main problem with subverting clichés is that they're out there waiting to be subverted. And in our post-ironic age, it's unlikely to find one that hasn't been twisted.

What's perhaps most interesting about these three varieties of Twitter wit is what they don't include: The ways to be clever on Twitter that are more recent inventions. There were only a smattering of celebrity comics back in 2009, among them Sarah Silverman and Michael Ian Black. The idea of tweeting as a character, whether fictional, historical or fake, is almost completely absent, save for the Tweet of God.

The 2009 collection also doesn't include hashtag games, a feature of Twitter that really makes the whole thing feel like a gigantic parlor game. Someone throws out the pound sign, a challenge—#LessInterestingBooks or #AddAWordRuin-AMovie—and an example to emulate, like "Waldo's Right Here" or "Live Gluten-Free or Die Hard." These games ripple through the Twitter universe, sometimes going into hibernation but rarely dying. They are both great wit sharpeners and exactly the sort of thing the Great Wits do to amuse themselves: For proof, we only need look to Christopher Hitchens's famous anecdote about a dinner party where the guests began imagining how Robert Ludlum—author of *The Bourne Identity*, *The Aquitaine Progression* and many more potboilers with similar titles—would have named Shakespeare's plays:

"At which point Salman Rushdie perked up and started to

#NOTJUSTFORTICTACTOE

sniff the air like a retriever," Hitchens recalled. "'O.K. then, Salman, what would *Hamlet*'s title be if submitted to the Ludlum treatment?' '*The Elsinore Vacillation,*' he replied—and I find I must stress this—in no more time than I have given you."

In a sense, all of Twitter has become a hashtag game that no longer even needs hashtags. That name we'll give it, for better or for worse: Thing, Meet Other Thing.

The Seinfeld Showdown

One of the most simultaneously comforting and depressing things about the Twitter universe is that you realize we all make the same jokes. When a joke-worthy event happens, the same line will occur to thousands of people around the world. This is where you see the true challenge to the modern wit: If you want "the strange assemblage of related ideas" in a way "that excites in the mind an agreeable surprise," you need only fire up Tweet-bot. There you'll find that much of the world is angling for the same assemblage, making it no longer strange but obvious and thus leaving the mind less than excited. Take, for example, the casting announcement of Ben Affleck as Batman, which happened at the same time as the Obama administration's public release of evidence that Syria had used chemical weapons. This resulted in countless tweets along the lines of "U.S. officials choose Ben Affleck to be the new Syria." The lesson here is clear: Before you tweet your clever wisecrack, take a second to see how many thousands of people have already made it. Next time, know that you have two options: To be faster, or to be more original. The latter is obviously preferable.

Since sometime after 2009, incongruous juxtaposition has been the order of the day on Twitter. Yes, it's spontaneous, but is it really unexpected if many people are doing it at once?

Perhaps the best distillation of this formula came from, of all places, the Obama campaign during the 2012 U.S. presidential election. As part of its outreach to the black community, the campaign used the slogan "I've got his back" with a picture of the back of the president's head. So when there was an opportunity to attack Mitt Romney's pledge to defund PBS, the Democrats whipped up a play on that ad featuring the familiar yellow-feathered back of Big Bird in place of the president's. The caption on the Tumblr said it all: "*Thing, meet other thing.*" Or as the Twitter joke formula goes, thing in the news, meet other thing in the news.

This isn't wit so much as a series of references. They demonstrate that you were paying attention and can spit back the trending topics of the day in different orders: Basically, that you're about as smart as the bots that outnumber humans on Twitter. Recall that when we were considering Oscar Wilde's weaker aphorisms, they all seemed like they could have been spat out by an algorithm. We're rapidly approaching the singularity of banal punch lines—not quite as scary as the Skynet scenario of the *Terminator* movies, though still unpleasant.

There is certainly some charm in the Twitter feeds of Kim

All too contrived.
This is obnoxious. Not funny.

Kierkegaardashian ("The philosophy of Søren Kierkegaard mashed with the tweets and observations of Kim Kardashian"), and by extension the same can be said of Justin Buber ("Combining the pop stylings of Justin Bieber with the existential wisdom of philosopher Martin Buber") and Kantye West ("The natural fusion of 18th Century Enlightenment Philosopher Immanuel Kant with tweets from Kanye West"). But that doesn't mean we have to like it, and it certainly doesn't mean it's wit.

Perhaps the apex of Thing Meet Other Thingism is Modern Seinfeld, the Twitter account that spits out plot synopses for an updated version of the 1990s sitcom. They are like diet soda: Pretty decent at first and reminiscent of the thing you liked, until you taste the artificial sweetness and realize just how cloying the whole formula is. To wit:

> @SeinfeldToday: Kramer starts an offline dating "site." KRAMER: It's like online dating . . . but at a place. JERRY: You're describing a bar! That's a bar!

> @SeinfeldToday: Elaine accidentally does a British accent in a job interview after marathoning Downton Abbey. She gets the job and has to keep faking it.

If you don't like these jokes, unfollow @SeinfeldToday. As the standard bearer for this school of tweets, it has an impeccable pedigree: One of its two creators worked for BuzzFeed, the site that took over the web by finding trending stories and shaping them into low-calorie listicles. You can't help but get sucked in, and then you wish you had helped. Again, maybe they get a pass. This is just a Twitter account, right?

This is where Twitter reveals itself to be both problem and solution. Hundreds of thousands of people deem Modern Seinfeld worth a follow, but tens of thousands opt instead (or also) for Seinfeld Current Day, the pitch-perfect parody of Modern Seinfeld. The low mental energy required to compute the former is taken down several notches to make the latter, which actually makes it brilliant. Character names are continually botched, misspellings are rampant, and the writer appears to have little familiarity with the show.

> @Seinfeld2000: Gerge name his baby iOS SEVEN

> @Seinfeld2000: 9/11 drcam makes jerry turn
> orthodox jewish but gives it up when he burps in
> church.

And perhaps most perfectly:

> @Seinfeld2000:
> Picture any thing
> K now imagen that thing in a diferent context
> LOL

In format and sophistication, this is an ideal introduction to Weird Twitter. It's hard to say exactly what it is other than a loosely defined subculture devoted to mocking and subverting the banal, obvious uses of the medium. Weird Tweeters make copious spelling mistakes, share dark jokes without punch lines and construct elaborate personas. In Peretti's definition of the simple service used by smart people, they are the smart-asses, the kids in the back of the class. But the mere fact they're there, invested in the medium, is encouraging. There's a good chance Twitter will become more and more homogenized, brand-driven and corporate; basically, that it will become Facebook. That may well kill Twitter wit. But as long as enough people deem it worthy of subverting, Twitter has a chance.

Twitter and You, or You Without Twitter

If we're going to tweet wittily, how do we do it? As luck would have it, a verified wit of our times has already drawn up the rules of engagement, so there's no need to study the private letters of Dorothy Parker for tips on whom to follow. Patton Oswalt sub-

mitted his rules for comedic tweeting to *GQ* magazine back in 2011, and indeed, if you follow them, you avoid all the pitfalls described thus far in this chapter. He starts with "be funny," which we'll admit is a noble goal but perhaps self-evident.

The good stuff begins with this: "Don't tweet to 'be there first.'" You won't be the first to make a super-obvious connection—a Thing Meet Other Thing moment—and we can add that even if you are there first, you can do better. You don't want to be the first crow to the dead gopher on the information superhighway. Aim higher.

He follows with "Don't overtweet," which is sound. A high proportion of deleted tweet drafts is a sign that you're teaching your brain to formulate the pithiest lines possible. You have nearly mastered the art of being interesting, and as a master you need quality control.

Then comes "Create a character," which is an interesting challenge but perhaps beyond the ambitions of non-comedians. Though you can certainly think of the persona you want to project, too much social-media identity tweaking eventually makes you a candidate for MTV's *Catfish*.

Finally, he advises comedians to "Pick fights with celebrities and corporations." Though corporate social-media strategies have evolved since 2011, there is still something deeply weird about companies with Twitter accounts, a weirdness best fought with Weird Twitter strategies. After all, why would you follow Holiday Inn? Aside from publicly registering complaints or perhaps the odd compliment, who wants to communicate with multinationals?

A nice example of this is the account of John Moe, the host of the public-radio show *Wits*. He has an ongoing fascination with Brawny paper towels, and indeed it doesn't take much to point out the inanity of a household cleaning product with a social-media presence. For instance:

> @Johnmoe: Disabusing you of the idea that you have "fans," towels. RT @BrawnyTowels: Happy Memorial Day, Brawny fans! What's on your agenda today?

Again, this might not be for everyone, but it's good to remember that as comfortable as all social networks can become, they aren't real life. There's a fourth wall there that's worth remembering and occasionally acknowledging.

Brevity IRL

But let's say you have no intention of joining Twitter, either because you don't see the point or because by the time this book is published it has already been exposed as a gigantic CIA sting operation, sort of like the way they funded patriotic literary magazines in the 1950s. Is there anything from this brave new world worth importing to your meek old world? Well, sure. All of Oswalt's guidelines are in some form applicable to witty conversation. Yes, you should be funny. No, don't say things just to say them first. "Don't overtweet" can be translated into "don't talk too much." As for character creation and mocking celebrities and corporations, well, it's good to be aware these are streams of modern thought that likely won't be contained to screens. You may well note that Twitter is itself a corporation.

Above all, remember the feature of Twitter that made it so attractive in the first place: Brevity. It's so intrinsic to the format that we haven't singled it out, but it's what allows so many people to be heard at once and form such a rich culture, one with its own heroes, villains, legends and paper-towel brands, in less than a decade. But as it's silly to expound on the merits of not expounding, let's wrap this up like so:

Brevity in Brief

Say less; mean more. Elements of wit don't get more elemental. If listeners think about what you've said for longer than it took you to say it, you've got the hang of this whole brevity thing. If minds wander while you're talking, you don't. And remember: Many of the greats never shut up; history was kind enough to distill their output. In real time, you need to do that for yourself.

{ QUIP QUIZ }

1. "Brevity is the soul of _____." —Dorothy Parker

2. "_____ is the soul of wit." —W. Somerset Maugham

3. "What is an epigram? A dwarfish whole. Its body brevity, and wit its _____." —Samuel Taylor Coleridge

4. "It's easy to assign less _____ to a pun than a poem—after all, laughter lightens the load."   **—Biz Stone**

5. "Every word is a _____ on silence."   **—Samuel Beckett**

Lingerie	Impropriety	Soul	Weight	Stain

Brevity wit List

☐ Don't be first, be best
☐ Keep it short
☐ are you still here?

Wit's End

If what we've been through is a sort of periodic table of wit, think of what follows as the fundamental properties of any atom of the stuff.

Wit takes work.

Not a single wit who has revealed his or her process contradicts this fact; those who have kept their methods opaque in all probability have this to hide. From George Bernard Shaw to Jay-Z, they spent years refining their material and, more important, the process by which they come up with material in the first place. It's a two-step technique: Find out what works, then find more of it. This is the caveat, one that hopefully won't apply to anyone who's come this far: There are individuals like those specimens in the Cornell studies of confidence who couldn't identify a funny line and compounded the misery by thinking they could. Unfortunately these people have mastered the black art of being interesting.

the witlifter

But it can't seem like work.

The Algonquin Round Table fell apart when attendees started showing up with obviously rehearsed one-liners and anecdotes. The only way to cheat at wit is by gaming the spontaneous part of *spontaneous creativity*. You do the wit work beforehand, properly identify when to deploy it and then—and this is everything— let it roll off your tongue like it's no big deal.

There's no formula for it.

This is the worst of Oscar Wilde infinitely multiplied by Twitter: If your witticism is a simple transposition of words, or a calculated mashing together of concepts, or anything that you could teach a computer to do, it's not wit. There's no gaming the system because as soon as you game it, you've lost. That said, you can likely get away with a few of these sorts of quips in a regular conversation. They're the Allen wrenches in your rhetorical toolkit: Extremely useful on rare occasions, unless you buy all your furniture from Ikea.

Unless you count the truth.

The only comedians we remember are the ones who were truth tellers. That sounds pretentious until you realize that Mitch Hedberg's observation that a severed foot is the ultimate stocking stuffer totally qualifies as the truth. An unconventional description of life is the surest path to wit.

And finally, to ensure we've distilled the Great Wits to their absolute essences, here are our lightning-round guides to using this book in everyday situations.

Wit at Work: The Cocktail Party

Remember Rebecca Northan's advice: No human isn't interesting. Then remember that she still discreetly screened the audience in the lobby before the show, factoring out the extremely shy and extremely outgoing. For everyone else, focus on being interested. And if you're offered a martini, ask yourself what Christopher Hitchens would do.

Wit at Work: Giving a Toast

Say you have a speech to give, a toast at a wedding or a presentation for work. Write it out beforehand, taking a few days to mull it over and select the best anecdotes and possible turns of phrase: Go the Full Churchill. Then divide it up into sections and memorize it by speaking it aloud a dozen times or more. When it comes time to speak, keep your notes in a pocket in case of emergency, but otherwise go from memory, linking the sections with impromptu observations if you feel comfortable doing so. And if anyone asks, say it was all off the cuff.

Wit at Work: Taking an Insult

Someone swears at you for cutting them off. You'd like to return fire, but what does that get you? Reach for Compassion instead—albeit in an ever-so-disingenuous way. "Thanks for the advice! Your feedback is helpful! Have a wonderful day!" This is practically guaranteed to destabilize someone expecting the middle finger, and what better way to get back at a boor? It's the Snappiest Comeback you can muster, and one you needn't think twice about if there are children within earshot.

Wit at Work: The Office Party

Don't overindulge. Do take the opportunity of seeing your colleagues in more casual surroundings to talk about subjects other than the perpetually jammed photocopier. Give those subjects a bit of thought ahead of time—just a modicum of hustle—so when you're at the bar ordering next to the guy from accounting, you can fill a few minutes.

Wit at Work: Meeting Your Prospective In-Laws

They're wondering if you're right for their son or daughter, and maybe you're not even sure yourself. Think of Oscar Wilde's Confidence: Of course, you'll make a wonderful spouse, and the two of you will do great things together! It only comes off as cocky if you don't live up to it. So live up to it. And by all means, don't name-drop Oscar Wilde.

Wit at Work: Talking to Kids

The one occasion on which it helps to know a few jokes, just in case. Try some open-ended questions, the sort that let the kid direct the conversation. Kids rarely get to control anything and are known to say the darnedest things, so it could go anywhere. If it goes nowhere, fall back on the jokes, or a selection of Ogden Nash poems.

Wit at Work: Dealing with Customer Service

Here, you are the righteous wit. Insulting the call-center employee is not going to win him over to your cause. Charm and compassion can make all the difference to someone who spends his or her workday dealing with irate customers. In addition to being basic human kindness, it may well also allow you to return that torn cardigan without a receipt.

Wit at Work: Writing a Thank-You Note

Remember Russell Brand's early discovery about how comedy works: "You have to train your mind to sift through the obvious stuff." The same applies here. Dinner was delicious, it was a pleasure to meet you, we appreciate the gift: These are platitudes, and as such, we read them without even processing what the words mean. If you're going to the trouble of sending a thank-you note, take a few minutes more to say something specific and original in it.

Wit at Work: The Job Interview

Hustle, hustle, hustle. Know everything you need to know about the industry, the company, the office and who will be interviewing you. When you get in there, flow. This advice may not work for all sectors, but if you're interviewing for Google and get one of their infamous questions—like, "Why are manhole covers round?"—wit is your best shot.

Wit at Work: The Eulogy

If ever there's an occasion to distinguish between jokes and wit, it's this one. Humor at a funeral is nearly impossible. A sparkling reminiscence of the departed, showcasing his best moments in a gentle glow, is what the occasion commands. As Nora Ephron said, "all painful things eventually turn into funny stories." Your job here is to smooth the way for this process, not by telling a funny story but by implicitly reminding everyone that the pain of the death won't always overshadow the joy of the life.

ACKNOWLEDGMENTS

From the initial idea to the final edits to the illustrations throughout, this book is entirely to the credit of Sarah Lazarovic. Except for the weaknesses, which are all mine and, to be fair, she knew about when she married me. I note with pride that her illustrated memoir, *A Bunch of Pretty Things I Did Not Buy*, has just been published by The Penguin Press and is, obviously, amazing.

Many friends, colleagues and mentors offered help along the way. Robert Fulford told me about Louis Kronenberger; Jacob Lazarovic pointed me toward Oscar Levant; Julie Bogdanowicz provided invaluable research assistance; Ben Kaplan went the distance; Tyler Hargreaves explained the perverse and often baffling role of wit in his many romantic successes; Maxime Lachance helped with translation, transliteration and transubstantiation; Ryan Allen fielded some of my legal questions; J. Kelly Nestruck clarified a few things about the theater; James S. F. Wilson brought his enormous erudition down upon an early draft like a sledgehammer on a gnat; Joshua Errett smoothed out the flow; and Barry Hertz proved that he is indeed part man, part machine, all editor.

My agent Sam Hiyate did his best with several variations of this book until it clicked, and my editor Marian Lizzi took the idea and, without any apparent effort, improved it immensely.

REFERENCES

INTRODUCTION

Studies in Words. C. S. Lewis. London: Cambridge University Press, 1960.

"The Wit in Large and Small Established Groups." Ewart E. Smith and Jacqueline D. Goodchilds. *Psychological Reports.* Aug. 1963, 13 (1): 273–274.

"The Wit and His Group." Jacqueline D. Goodchilds and Ewart E. Smith. *Human Relations.* Jan. 1964, 17.23–31.

"Wit, Creativity and Sarcasm." Ewart E. Smith and Helen L. White. *Journal of Applied Psychology.* Apr. 1965, 9(2): 131–134.

"The Wit: A Personality Analysis." John F. Clabby Jr. *Journal of Personality Assessment.* June 1980, 44 (3): 307–310.

"The Creativity Crisis." Po Bronson. *Newsweek.* July 10, 2010.

Creativity: Flow and the Psychology of Discovery and Invention. Mihaly Csikszentmihalyi. New York: HarperPerennial, 1997.

A Smile in the Mind. Beryl McAlhone and David Stuart. London: Phaidon Press, 1988.

HUSTLE

"Downsize," *The Office.* BBC. July 9, 2001. Television.

"Homer vs. Dignity," *The Simpsons.* Fox. Nov. 26, 2000. Television.

Lord Malquist & Mr. Moon. Tom Stoppard. London: Faber & Faber, 1966.

My Early Life: 1874–1904. Winston Churchill. New York: Charles Scribner's Sons, 1930.

Churchill by Himself: The Definitive Collection of Quotations. Richard Langworth, ed. New York: PublicAffairs, 2008.

"Jonathan's Jokes: American Humour in the Late-Victorian Press." Bob Nicholson. *Media History.* 2012, 18(1): 33–49.

"Maybe I Can Impress Her with My *Holy Grail* Quotes." *Onion,* theonion.com. Oct. 11, 2000.

The Quote Verifier: Who Said What, Where and When. Ralph Keyes. New York: St. Martin's, 2006.

You Might as Well Live: The Life and Times of Dorothy Parker. John Keats. New York: Paragon House, 1970.

"How to Be Handsomely Witty?" ask.metafilter.com. June 2, 2007.

"Mixed Blessings." *The Golden Girls.* NBC. Mar. 19, 1988. Television.

"Seddit, How Do You Improve Your Wit?" reddit.com. Jan. 26, 2013.

FLOW

"Discovery-Oriented Behavior and the Originality of Creative Products: A Study with Artists." Mihaly Csikszentmihalyi and J. W. Getzels. *Journal of Personality and Social Psychology.* July 1971, 19(1): 47–52.

"The Americanization of Rock Climbing." Mihaly Csikszentmihalyi. *University of Chicago Magazine.* 1969, 61(6): 20–27.

Book of Rhymes: The Poetics of Hip Hop. Adam Bradley. New York: BasicCivitas, 2009.

"It's Not About You." David Brooks. *New York Times.* May 30, 2011.

Flow: The Psychology of Optimal Experience. Mihaly Csikszentmihalyi. New York: HarperPerennial, 1990.

Decoded. Jay-Z (Shawn Carter). New York: Spiegel & Grau, 2010.

Empire State of Mind. Zach O'Malley Greenburg. New York: Penguin Portfolio, 2007.

"The Meeting with a President and a 'King,'" Dave "Davey D" Cook, in *Jay-Z: Essays on Hip Hop's Philosopher King.* Julius Bailey, ed. Jefferson, N.C.: McFarland, 2011.

"The Book of Jay." Touré. *Rolling Stone.* No. 989, Dec. 15, 2005.

"Neural Correlates of Lyrical Improvisation: An fMRI Study of Freestyle Rap." Siyuan Liu, Ho Ming Chow, Yisheng Xu, Michael G. Erkkinen, Katherine E. Swett, Michael W. Eagle, Daniel A. Rizik-Baer and Allen R. Braun. *Scientific Reports.* Nov. 15, 2012.

INTUITION

Truth in Comedy: The Manual of Improvisation. Charna Halpern, Del Close and Kim "Howard" Johnson. Colorado Springs: Meriwether Publishing, 1994.

Wit and Its Relation to the Unconscious. Sigmund Freud. A. A. Brill, trans. New York: Moffat, Yard, 1916.

Leo Rosten's Carnival of Wit: From Aristotle to Woody Allen. New York: Plume, 1994.

A Smattering of Ignorance. Oscar Levant. New York: Bartholomew House, 1939.

The Memoirs of an Amnesiac. Oscar Levant. New York: Putnam, 1965.

A Talent for Genius: The Life and Times of Oscar Levant. Sam Kashner and Nancy Schoenberger. New York: Villard, 1994.

Love, Groucho: Letters from Groucho Marx to His Daughter Miriam. Miriam Marx Allen, ed. London: Faber & Faber, 1992.

"Writer's Block Can Be a Beautiful Thing." Alex Beam. *Boston Globe*, Jan. 6, 2004.

"Too Easy Does It: Can Revelling in Laziness Really Be a Creative Respite?" Mark Medley. *National Post*, Apr. 22, 2008.

"Keith Olbermann: What I've Learned." Interview by Cal Fussman, Sept. 17, 2013. *Esquire*. Dec. 2013.

"He's in Tune." Michael Arace. Hartford *Courant*. Sept. 28, 1993.

"Martin Amis, The Art of Fiction No. 151." Interviewed by Francesca Riviere. *Paris Review*. No. 146. Spring 1998.

Born Standing Up: A Comic's Life. Steve Martin. New York: Scribner, 2007.

CONFIDENCE

"Are We All Less Risky and More Skillful Than Our Fellow Drivers?" Ola Svenson. *Acta Psychologica*. Feb. 1981, 7(2): 143–148.

"Unskilled and Unaware of It: How Difficulties in Recognizing One's Own Incompetence Lead to Inflated Self-Assessments." Justin Kruger and David Dunning. *Journal of Personality and Social Psychology*. Dec. 1999, 77(6): 1121–1134.

My Memoirs. Sir Francis Robert Benson. London: Ernest Benn, 1930.

Oscar Wilde. Richard Ellmann. New York: Vintage, 1988.

Oscar's Books: A Journey Around the Library of Oscar Wilde. Thomas Wright. London: Vintage, 2009.

Oscar Wilde. Louis Kronenberger. Boston: Little, Brown, 1976.

The Collected Works of W. B. Yeats, Vol. VI: Prefaces and Introductions. William Butler Yeats. New York: Scribner, 1990.

"Self-Plagiarism, Creativity and Craftsmanship in Oscar Wilde." Josephine M. Guy. *English Literature in Transition, 1880–1920*. 1998, 41(1): 6–23.

REFRESHMENT

Baja Oklahoma. Dan Jenkins. New York: Atheneum, 1982.

Intoxication and Society. Philip Withington. Referenced in "England's Booze
Culture: Always with Us." *Economist*. Dec. 31, 2011.

Life as I Find It: A Treasury of Mark Twain Rarities. Charles Neider, ed. Lanham,
Md.: Cooper Square Publishers, 2000.

How's Your Glass?: Quizzical Looks at Drinks and Drinking. Kingsley Amis. London:
Arrow Books, 1985.

The Quotable Hitchens: From Alcohol to Zionism. Christopher Hitchens. Windsor
Mann, ed. Cambridge, Mass.: Da Capo, 2011.

Hitch-22: A Memoir. Christopher Hitchens. New York: Twelve Books, 2010.

"He Knew He Was Right." Ian Parker. *New Yorker*. Oct. 16, 2006.

"208: Office Politics." David Rakoff. *This American Life*. Thisamericanlife.com.
WBEZ. Mar. 15, 2002.

The Wit & Wisdom of Oscar Wilde: A Treasury of Quotations, Anecdotes, and Repartee.
Ralph Keyes. New York: HarperCollins, 1996.

RIGHTEOUSNESS

"Louis C.K.'s DIY TV." James Poniewozik. *Time*. June 26, 2011. (Plus full interview
transcript, published in two parts on time.com.)

Shameless. Louis C.K. stand-up special. HBO Films, 2007.

Chewed Up. Louis C.K. stand-up special. Showtime, 2008.

Hilarious. Louis C.K. stand-up special. 2010.

Lives of the Wits. Hesketh Pearson. London: Heinemann, 1962.

George Bernard Shaw: His Life and Works—A Critical Biography. Archibald Hender-
son. Cincinnati: Stewart & Kidd, 1911.

Modern Critical Views: George Bernard Shaw. Harold Bloom, ed. New York: Chelsea
House, 1987. (Includes Stanley Weintraub's helpful essay "Introduction to
Shaw." Originally printed in *The Portable Bernard Shaw*. New York: Viking,
1977.)

Bernard Shaw: The One-Volume Definitive Edition. Michael Holroyd. New York:
Random House, 1988.

CHARM

"Cary Grant's Suit." Todd McEwen. *Granta 94: On the Road Again*. Summer
2006.

"The Man from Dream City." Pauline Kael. *New Yorker*. July 14, 1975.

"Forget Da Vinci, How's Iceland?" Robert W. Welkos. *Los Angeles Times*. May 23, 2006.

"RD3." Chris Heath. *GQ*. Apr. 2013.

"Boris Johnson 'Would Like to Be PM.'" BBC. Mar. 19, 2013.

"Trust Me, Being Sacked Isn't All Bad." Boris Johnson. *Daily Telegraph*. Dec. 2, 2004.

"So, Bumbling Boris Johnson Is Loveable and Funny? Well, Have I Got News for You." Sonia Purnell. *Observer*. Aug. 5, 2012.

"Why Am I Asking Boris Johnson to Marry Me." Van Badham. *Guardian*. Aug. 22, 2013.

ROMANCE Women are ~~funny~~ plenty funny, but in a different way

"Why Women Aren't Funny." Christopher Hitchens. *Vanity Fair*. Jan. 2007.

"Why We Laugh—Or Do We?" From *The Benchley Roundup: A Selection by Nathaniel Benchley of His Favorites*. New York: Harper, 1954.

My Booky Wook. Russell Brand. London: Hodder & Stoughton, 2007.

Booky Wook 2: This Time It's Personal. Russell Brand. London: HarperCollins, 2010.

Morning Joe. MSNBC. New York. June 17, 2013.

Mae West: An Icon in Black and White. Jill Watts. New York: Oxford University Press, 2001.

Mae West: It Ain't No Sin. Simon Louvish. New York: St. Martin's, 2005.

RESILIENCE

"The Comeback." *Seinfeld*. NBC. Jan. 30, 1997.

Al Jaffee's Mad Life. Mary-Lou Weisman. New York: It Books, 2010.

Nora Ephron interview. Academy of Achievement, achievement.org. June 21, 2007.

"Nora Ephron: The Heroine of Her Life, Not the Victim." Jane Shilling. *Daily Telegraph*. June 27, 2012.

Autobiography of Mark Twain, Vol. 2. Benjamin Griffin and Harriet Elinor Smith, eds. Berkeley: University of California Press, 2013.

My Life with Groucho: A Son's Eye View. Arthur Marx. New York: Simon & Schuster, 1954.

The Essential Groucho: Writings by, for and about Groucho Marx. Stefan Kanfer, ed. New York: Vintage, 2000.

"Bob Hope and Groucho Marx Run a Radio Station." *The Walgreen Hour* (radio). Mar. 27, 1947.

COMPASSION

The Annotated Hunting of the Snark: The Definitive Edition. Lewis Carroll. Martin Gardner, ed. New York: Norton, 2006.

"Ricky Gervais and the British Way." *Economist.* Jan. 18, 2011.

"On Smarm." Tom Scocca. Gawker.com. Dec. 5, 2013.

Laughter's Gentle Soul: The Life of Robert Benchley. Billy Altman. New York: Norton, 1997.

Robert Benchley: His Life and Good Times. Babette Rosmond. New York: Paragon, 1970.

Ogden Nash: The Life and Work of America's Laureate of Light Verse. Douglas M. Parker, with foreword by Dana Gioia. Chicago: Ivan R. Dee, 2005.

The Best of Ogden Nash: 548 Favorite Poems from America's Laureate of Light Verse. Linell Nash Smith, ed. Chicago: Ivan R. Dee, 2007.

CONVERSATION

Rebecca Northan spoke to me in early 2014. You can find out more about her work at northan.com and follow her on Twitter @rebeccanorthan.

"Fran Lebowitz, a Humorist at Work." James Linville and George Plimpton, interviewers. *Paris Review.* No. 127. Summer 1993.

Great Times, Good Times: The Odyssey of Maurice Barrymore. James Kotsilibas-Davis. New York: Knopf, 1977.

"Maurice Barrymore's Dilemma: From *Harper's Weekly*." *New York Times.* Jan. 9, 1905.

Wit's End: Days and Nights of the Algonquin Round Table. James R. Gaines. New York: Harcourt Brace Jovanovich, 1977.

The Algonquin Wits. Robert E. Drennan, ed. New York: Citadel Press, 1990.

"Tom Stoppard and Michael Holroyud Interview Themselves." *Royal Society of Literature Review,* 2005, via rslit.org.

"Tom Stoppard Nonstop: Word Games with a Hit Playwright." Jon Bradshaw. *New York.* Jan. 10, 1977, pp. 47–51.

BREVITY

Twitter Wit: Brilliance in 140 Characters or Less. Nick Douglas, ed. New York: It Books, 2009.

"Assassins of the Mind." Christopher Hitchens. *Vanity Fair.* Feb. 2009.

"Patton Oswalt's Guide to Not Sucking at Twitter." Patton Oswalt. *GQ.* Aug. 2011.

Glimpse: Selected Aphorisms. George Murray. Toronto: ECW Press, 2007.

INDEX

Page numbers in *italics* indicate illustrations.